PURE
VANILLA

PURE VANILLA

IRRESISTIBLE RECIPES and ESSENTIAL TECHNIQUES

by SHAUNA SEVER

photography by
LEIGH BEISCH

Library of Congress Cataloging in Publication Number: 2011946058

ISBN: 978-1-59474-596-6
Printed in China
Typeset in YWFT Victoria and Grotesque
Designed by Sugar
Art direction by Katie Hatz
Photography by Leigh Beisch
Prop styling by Sara Slavin
Production management by John J. McGurk

Quirk Books
215 Church St.
Philadelphia, PA 19106
quirkbooks.com
10 9 8 7 6 5 4 3

INTRODUCTION

VANILLA: ANYTHING BUT ORDINARY

"How was your date?"

"Ugh...he was so vanilla."

Boring. Plain Jane. Vanilla sex, Vanilla Coke, plain vanilla interest-rate swaps. *Vanilla Ice*, for crying out loud.

Poor vanilla. Poor underestimated vanilla. For years, the word has meant anything but interesting, complex, or exotic. And why? It's probably mostly Vanilla Ice's fault, but still...

Even with a history as rich as hers, poor vanilla is too often overlooked and misunderstood, a mere afterthought in recipes. Is it because we've taken this lush, soft spice for granted for so long? Been comforted and soothed by her simplicity and her quiet, sweet manner to the point that we consider her only a supporting character and never the star? Hundreds of cookbooks wax poetic about her sexy, super-popular sister chocolate, while vanilla watches longingly from the sidelines, quietly waiting for her due in the culinary world.

Personally, I'll never understand indifference about vanilla, the way some people skip right over it and hurtle straight for the chocolate. Of course, we all have moments when we need a hunk of chocolate and nothing else will do, but I've always been a Vanilla Person. Loud and proud, I am Totally Vanilla. I'll take vanilla bean ice cream over chocolate explosion any day of the week. Even the most mundane restaurant dessert menu can excite me if a venerable crème brûlée is included along with the chocolate lava cake and the apple crisp. I've never thought of vanilla as being, well, "vanilla." It's high time to catapult this delicious ingredient into the superstar stratosphere where she so deserves to be!

Vanilla is the world's most universally loved flavor, and for good reason. No flavor is more widely recognized, used, and enjoyed across the globe. Worldwide, vanilla ice cream sales consistently top other flavors at least 2 to 1. Vanilla extract is in just about every imaginable baked good. Even chocolate contains vanilla, which heightens its chocolaty flavor. Vanilla, it seems, is more versatile and dynamic than just about any foodstuff out there, and yet it's synonymous with the plainest, most boring things. No fair!

This book aims to change all that. In these pages, we'll explore so much more than just a great vanilla ice cream recipe. We'll travel through the story of vanilla, from its start as a green pod nestled inside a tropical flower to its transformation into the fragrant beans we all recognize and love. Finally, we'll dive into a collection of creamy, cakey, buttery, sweet, and even a few savory recipes that all celebrate the unmistakably dreamy flavor of vanilla—and are anything but ordinary. We're about to lift this humble culinary background player to icon status.

Homemade Vanilla Extract
and Vanilla Sugar, recipes
page 87 and 69.

A BRIEF HISTORY OF VANILLA

The history of the vanilla bean is every bit as rich and complex as its flavor. It begins with the **Totonac Indians of Mexico**, who discovered the vanilla orchid and its precious pods more than two thousand years ago. Totonac mythology tells the tale of the anguished princess Xanat, forbidden by her father to marry a mortal. After escaping with her secret lover, the two were captured and beheaded in a bloody massacre, and in the soil where their blood fell, the vine of a vanilla orchid began to bloom. Drama! Intrigue! And that's only a tiny fraction of the fascinating history of the vanilla bean.

1519 **THE AZTECS CONQUER THE TOTONAC INDIANS,** who are credited with having discovered, cured, and consumed vanilla many years earlier. The Totonacs introduce their techniques to the Aztecs, who popularize the use of vanilla throughout Mexico and Central America.

1519 **SPANISH CONQUISTADOR HERNÁN CORTÉS ARRIVES IN MEXICO.** Wined and dined by the Aztec emperor Montezuma, Cortés is blown away by the flavor of vanilla that he tastes in many Aztec dishes, particularly a very early, and very bitter, version of hot chocolate. Although the vanilla bean was known in Europe several years earlier, it was used only as a perfume until Cortés enthusiastically brought the beans back to Spain and shared their "newfound" edible uses.

early 1600s

THE TREND OF FLAVORING BEVERAGES AND DESSERTS WITH VANILLA BEANS finds favor with the European upper class, namely Queen Elizabeth I, who is known to have a legendary sweet tooth. Vanilla establishes itself as a star flavor in custards, puddings, and cakes, especially in France and Italy.

late 1600s

VANILLA FALLS OUT OF FAVOR IN SPAIN, displaced by cinnamon, a cheaper and more widely available flavoring. But vanilla continues to gain popularity in France, where advanced pastry-making techniques are being developed. In fact, it becomes so popular that the French try to grow their own vanilla orchids on the French colony of Bourbon Island (now called Réunion). The flowers fail to produce pods, and the mystery of how the Mexicans successfully grew vanilla for centuries remains intact.

1789

THOMAS JEFFERSON, THEN U.S. AMBASSADOR TO FRANCE, FALLS IN LOVE WITH THE FLAVOR OF VANILLA and carries a bundle of beans home to Monticello. A gourmand and ice-cream-making fanatic with a voracious appetite for sweets, Jefferson is often credited with introducing vanilla to Americans. He impresses guests with his vanilla desserts served at elaborate dinner parties; today his vanilla ice cream recipe is stored in the Library of Congress in Washington, D.C.

1836

BELGIAN BOTANIST CHARLES MORREN DISCOVERS that vanilla orchids aren't self-pollinating and that certain species of bees and hummingbirds indigenous to Mexico are responsible for the plant yielding fruit. Morren then develops an extremely tedious method of hand-pollinating the flowers.

1837 BOSTON PHARMACIST JOSEPH BURNETT DEVELOPS
THE EARLIEST METHOD FOR PRODUCING VANILLA
EXTRACT, making the spice much more widely available
in liquid form.

1841 EDMOND ALBIUS, THE TWELVE-YEAR-OLD SON OF A SLAVE
ON RÉUNION, IS CREDITED WITH devising a much more
efficient and productive way of hand-pollinating vanilla orchids
with a long, thin wooden rod; his method is still in use today.
His discovery paves the way for this Indian Ocean region
(including Réunion and its larger neighbor, Madagascar) to
become the world's largest producer of vanilla, often exported
under the name Bourbon.

present **DAY** VANILLA REMAINS THE WORLD'S FAVORITE FLAVOR.
Americans are responsible for consuming roughly half of all
vanilla produced globally; the spice is consumed mainly in
ice cream and sodas. The cosmetics industry also is a huge
consumer of vanilla, using it to scent products and perfumes.

FROM ORCHID TO EXTRACT

Have you ever picked up a small vial of vanilla beans and been gobsmacked by the high price? Well, you're not alone. Vanilla beans are the world's second most expensive spice, right behind saffron (whose little red threads are in fact the painstakingly hand-harvested stamens of crocuses, hardly an easy day's work). But when you take into consideration the astonishing amount of time, effort, and work that harvesting vanilla requires, its staggering price tag doesn't seem so unreasonable.

The brown, leathery, oily, and unbelievably fragrant beans that we call vanilla start out as relatively flavorless, odorless green seedpods hanging in the center of certain species of flowering orchids. The plants' blooms look pretty similar to the ones on the orchids you see decorating the pages of furniture catalogs and available for purchase in greenhouses. But vanilla orchids are a little different: they can be grown only under specific conditions, namely, in hot, humid, tropical locations that are about 700 to 1,400 miles from the equator. These climatic requirements limit the plants' availability, as does the flowers' rare appearance—vanilla orchids bloom just once a year.

Vanilla orchid vines need room to roam, so the plants are often found on large plantations that are expensive to maintain. Left to grow wild, vanilla orchids will climb up any available tree or support. For cultivation purposes, vanilla growers expertly guide the vines to maintain a height accessible for hand harvesting. In fact, the entire process of growing and harvesting vanilla must be done manually—and that's the main reason it's so expensive. Here's how the cycle breaks down:

HARVEST. When the blooms first open, farmers have just twelve hours to hand-pollinate each one in order to get the seedpods to develop. The pods themselves take ten months to mature. Once the pods have grown, they must be carefully harvested by hand and at precisely the right growing stage. Because of the fierce competition in the world of vanilla, particularly in Madagascar, some producers may burn each green pod with "vanilla tattoos," a sort of branding technique that indicates who the individual grower is and prevents the beans from changing hands before they can be cured and shipped by the rightful owners. The tattoos are obvious on cured vanilla beans, appearing as light, blistered areas. (You can see evidence of this on page 156.) The next four stages make up the curing part of the process and can take another six to eight months to complete.

KILLING. After the pods are plucked from the orchids, they're "killed," meaning that they're prevented from further development. Most often, this is done by submersion in a hot bath, though in some places, especially Mexico, pods are sun killed. The killing stage is the first step toward developing the flavor and aroma of a vanilla bean, but additional curing is what really intensifies the flavor. Curing is an impressive, time-consuming feat. To sound all fancy and scientific: it encourages an enzymatic reaction in the pod that produces a substance called vanillin. Nonscientifically speaking, vanillin is what gives vanilla its delicious flavor and yummy smell.

SWEATING. After the pods are killed, they're sweated, or stored for a week or two packed in cozy layers of cloth or wool blankets in a high-humidity environment. During this stage, the pods oxidize and take on most of their characteristic brown color.

DRYING. The approximately month-long drying stage removes most of the remaining moisture from the pods. The method for drying varies based on the producer—it can be sun drying, indoor drying, or a combination of the two.

CONDITIONING. Finally comes the crucial conditioning stage, a six-month rest in well-packed boxes during which a vanilla bean develops its deep, heady, swoon-worthy fragrance. This is the "supermodeling" of the bean, if you will.

The finished beans are then sorted and graded according to their length and quality. Grade A (also called "prime" or "gourmet") beans are the plumpest and most beautiful and also the longest (greater length corresponds to higher vanillin content, which means extra vanilla fragrance and flavor). Grade A beans are packaged to be sold whole.

Grade B beans, also called "extract beans," are most often sold for use in extracts and other vanilla products.

VANILLA IN ALL ITS FORMS

Obviously, I'm a bit of a vanilla fanatic, but even I was surprised to learn that there's more to vanilla than just beans and extracts. Vanilla comes in a variety of forms, and each has its own unique qualities. In a pinch, you can substitute one for another without significant difference or loss of flavor (for equivalents, see the handy chart on the inside front cover). Still, whenever possible, I prefer to use the type of vanilla best suited for the recipe I'm making. That way, I know I'm getting the most bang for my buck and, more important, the purest vanilla flavor.

WHOLE VANILLA BEANS are the brown, fragrant seedpods from which all vanilla goodness comes. Look for beans that are glossy, a bit oily, dark in color, and supple enough to be wrapped around your finger without splitting or snapping.

When you slice open that gorgeous pod, you'll find innumerable teeny black seeds, known as vanilla caviar. As beautiful as those black flecks are, they don't impart a ton of flavor. It's the pod that carries most of the dreamy flavor and fragrance. I tend to use whole beans only in recipes that offer the opportunity to steep a pod in hot liquid, as for a custard, an ice cream base, or a beverage. I split the bean lengthwise and throw it in the pot to heat up along with the liquid. I don't bother scraping the bean before adding it to the pot; instead, I wait until it's steeped, which makes the bean plump and tender, and then scrape the caviar into the liquid. This makes it much easier to remove the seeds, leaving the fibrous threads behind.

If you choose to use the caviar without first steeping the bean, be sure to save the pod to make things like vanilla sugar, homemade extract, and infused liquors (for directions, see pages 69, 87, and 151). Even steeped and scraped pods can be rinsed, dried thoroughly, and used two or three more times. Let your nose be your guide: when a bean doesn't smell like much anymore, it's time to retire it.

PURE VANILLA EXTRACT, the fragrant liquid in that little brown bottle we all know and love, is endlessly versatile. It is made by steeping vanilla beans in alcohol, the best substance for pulling out all that rich flavor. Another extraction method is percolation, the same process used in a coffeemaker, in which the alcohol is held in a reservoir and continually pumped over the vanilla beans and then drained. After extraction, most manufacturers give the liquid time to age and mellow—usually a few months but sometimes up to two years—before bottling.

To be labeled "pure," vanilla extract must contain at least 0.11 grams of vanillin per 100 milliliters and 35 percent alcohol (the percentage is printed on the label). The best applications for extracts are those recipes involving high heat, as for baked goods, so that most of the alcohol can evaporate, leaving behind just the sweet vanilla flavor.

The key to buying the best vanilla extract is to read the label carefully. Look for the phrase "pure vanilla extract" and avoid anything that says "imitation" or "vanilla flavoring" (see page 24 for more information). To help the extract reach its full potential in a recipe, beat it into the fat as early as possible; for example, if you're creaming together butter and sugar, add the vanilla then, rather than when you add eggs or wet ingredients. This trick is good for preserving the character of any spice or flavoring, but it's especially helpful when working with extracts and pastes. Fat traps and carries flavor, which prevents the vanilla from baking off and encourages it to blossom when exposed to heat.

VANILLA BEAN PASTE, one of my favorite vanilla products, gives a one-two punch of the intense flavor of an extract plus the aesthetic beauty of all those vanilla caviar flecks (minus the investment in pricey pods). It's a great time-saver, too: no need to scrape the bean.

VANILLA POWDER is the stuff in the shakers near the sweeteners and stirrers at coffee bars. Typically, it's made from vanilla extract or flavoring plus some kind of starch, like maltodextrin. Higher-quality powders may also contain finely ground whole beans, giving them a brownish tinge; these are flavorful enough to be used in baked goods. Low-quality powders are white and tend to taste more like whatever starch they're made with. Price is an indicator of quality; expensive varieties are likely to contain more vanilla. To incorporate into baking recipes, sift the vanilla powder right into the other dry ingredients. I like to use vanilla powder to make a sort of quick vanilla sugar, whisking it with granulated sugar and sprinkling it on dishes for a fragrant, frosty finish (see Vanilla Bean Bread Pudding, page 31).

GROUND VANILLA is one of the lesser-known forms, and an interesting one at that. Not to be confused with vanilla powder, this stuff is in fact ground whole beans; it comes packaged in tiny jars. Because it contains both the ground-up pod and the vanilla caviar, its flavor is even stronger than that of vanilla bean paste. Additionally, flecks of ground vanilla are a bit larger than vanilla caviar, making it perfect for rustic, textured baked goods in which caviar alone would get lost.

VANILLA ORIGINS, VARIETIES, AND TASTING NOTES

For most of us, our vanilla experiences are limited to the little brown bottle we buy in the supermarket. But that's really just the beginning. I like to compare the world of vanilla to that of wine—there are several fascinating varieties and flavor profiles out there, and learning the basics will help you truly celebrate it and get the most for your money.

Continuing with the oenological analogy, imagine a row of glasses containing different red wines all lined up on a table. At first glance, without swirling the glasses or holding them up to the light, it's hard to see much difference among the wines. But pick up a glass, take a whiff, and taste, and you'll start to notice each wine's nuances. That's exactly the way different varieties (and forms) of vanilla show their true colors.

Some vanilla enthusiasts speak of vanilla's *terroir*, or how the soil and growing conditions contribute to the beans' characteristics. The way beans are handled and cured after harvesting also influences each product's unique fragrances and flavors. These distinctions among the varieties are as noticeable in whole bean form as they are in extracts. (To investigate these differences for yourself, check out "Throw a Vanilla Tasting Party," page 116.)

Just as there are many types of winemaking grapes, there are different species of vanilla orchids, as many as 150 worldwide. Of these 150 species, only three are edible, and just two of them are commonly used in the kitchen.

VANILLA PLANIFOLIA is the most popular species of vanilla—most commercially available vanilla beans and extracts are members of this species. *V. planifolia* varieties are named after their place of origin, of which there are many, and each origin has its own unique characteristics. This species is grown in many countries, chiefly Madagascar, Indonesia, and Mexico, as well as on a smaller scale in places like Costa Rica, Jamaica, Hawaii, and China. To show the impressive range of flavors and fragrances produced by different growing locations, here are some of its most notable places of origin:

 MADAGASCAR: Also called Madagascar Bourbon or Bourbon vanilla, not because it contains booze but because it's named after neighboring Bourbon Island—now known as Réunion—where the methods of cultivating vanilla were refined and perfected. It is endlessly versatile and has the sort of rich, creamy, sweet flavor most of us associate with vanilla. Because of its wide availability and familiar flavor, most people consider Madagascar vanilla to be the Mother of All Vanillas.

BOURBON: This term is often used interchangeably with Madagascar vanilla but may refer specifically to vanilla from Réunion.

MEXICO: If there's a loyalty war in the vanilla world, it's mostly likely between Team Mexico and Team Madagascar. Mexico is the birthplace of the vanilla plant. In fact, for hundreds of years before the development of hand-pollination techniques, vanilla was grown only in Mexico and Central America, where the flowers were fertilized by a specific species of bee found only in that part of the world. Because of this rare combination of orchids and just the right kind of bees to pollinate them, Mexico ruled the world's vanilla production for centuries, until a frost in the mid-1950s destroyed much of the harvest.

Many of the traditional methods for processing beans in Mexico are still used today, and they give Mexican vanilla its signature smooth, complex quality, with hints of spices like cloves and nutmeg. Unlike water-killed Madagascar pods, Mexican vanillas are traditionally killed in the sun, which contributes to their wonderful woodsy flavor and aroma.

INDONESIA: Because it is intense in both flavor and aroma, some people find this variety too harsh and smoky, bordering on unpleasantly strong. The intensity of Indonesian beans is ideal for rich recipes made with lots of butterfat or cream, and recipes that are cooked or baked at high heat. Most often, Indonesian beans are blended with Bourbon beans and used for extract rather than being sold whole.

INDIA: A quick sniff suggests that Indian vanilla beans are similar to their Madagascar and Bourbon cousins. But these beans are visually impressive: noticeably plumper than other varieties, with a ton of seeds and super-dark-brown pods. Despite their sweet fragrance, the flavor of Indian beans is smoky, with a hint of bittersweet chocolate.

UGANDA: Like Indian beans, vanilla beans from Uganda are of notable size, though typically their color is not quite so dark. Incredibly potent and bold, with a sweet, winey, raisinlike fragrance and flavor, they are perfect for rich desserts, especially ones containing chocolate.

TONGA: Grown on the teeny island of Tonga in the South Pacific, these beans have the most savory qualities compared to other vanillas, making them a no-brainer for dressings, marinades, and similar dishes (like Vanilla, Brown Sugar, and Black Pepper Bacon, page

32). Chocolate makers like Tonga vanilla's bold, pronounced characteristics and notes of fig and bark, which are a perfect complement to intense, bittersweet flavors. Since Tonga produces a relatively small amount of beans with unique qualities, these are rare and prized.

VANILLA TAHITENSIS is a dreamboat and in a class of its own. Commonly known as Tahitian vanilla, this species comes in far fewer varieties than *V. planifolia*. Some researchers suspect that it might be a hybrid of two different vanilla plants. Today, some Tahitian vanilla is still grown in Tahiti, but, surprisingly, most comes from Papua New Guinea. This species has a beautiful, ambrosial quality, with intense fruity, floral notes that are often cherrylike in flavor and fragrance. The pods have thicker walls and fewer seeds than those of other species, making them excellent for steeping.

Tahitian vanilla is lower in vanillin than *V. planifolia*, which allows its outstanding fruity and floral qualities to come forward. These characteristics make Tahitian vanilla ideal for pairing with fruits of all sorts and excellent in custards and creams, where it can be the star. Tahitian vanilla is less likely to be used as a supporting character or background note in a recipe, as a Madagascar Bourbon extract might. It is a vanilla-dessert lover's dream. *V. pompona* is a lesser-known edible type. Also known as West Indian vanilla, this species is grown throughout the Caribbean and Central and South America.

Just as wines can be paired with certain foods, there is an art to pairing vanilla varieties and forms with recipes that allow them to truly shine. Armed with this knowledge, you can get the most for the precious bucks you shell out for this expensive spice. After years of knowing nothing more about vanilla than that brown bottle from the supermarket, it's exciting to learn about the fragrances and flavors of individual varieties from all over the world.

VANILLA FAQS

Why is vanilla so expensive? Few food products require the amount of time, special growing conditions, and careful work by human hands that is needed to transform vanilla from its natural state into those beans and extracts on store shelves. That translates to hefty prices, especially for high-quality brands. For this reason, I usually buy my vanilla products online from trusted sources (see Resources, page 157).

What does it mean when a vanilla label says "two-fold," "three-fold," "four-fold," etc.? This is an indication of the product's intensity and concentration. With extract, for example, rules dictate how many vanilla beans must be used to make 1 gallon of extract (in the United States, that amount is at least 13.35 ounces). So, there is twice that weight of beans in a batch of two-fold vanilla extract, three times the weight in three-fold extract, and so on. Most pure vanilla extracts are single-fold; food manufacturers tend to use higher concentrations. But if you do come across a highly concentrated specialty vanilla product, you may want to reduce slightly the amount that a recipe calls for, to keep it from becoming overpowering.

How do I store vanilla? Extracts, pastes, powders, and ground beans are best stored in dark-colored, tightly capped jars. Whole beans should be tightly wrapped in plastic wrap and then placed in a zip-top bag to help retain moisture. Like any spice, vanilla in any form is best kept in a cool, dark place. Don't store whole beans in the fridge—it might seem like a logical place, but in fact the damp conditions tend to encourage mold growth on the seedpods.

How long will whole beans keep? Tightly wrapped, whole beans can keep for up to a year. If they dry out, you can rehydrate them by soaking briefly in hot water. However, dried beans are still perfectly useable for steeping in hot liquids or for making vanilla sugar (see page 69).

How long will vanilla extract keep? Because of its high alcohol content, when stored in a cool, dark place, pure vanilla extract will keep for years. But I hope you use it up a lot more quickly than that!

My vanilla pods have white crystals on them—have they gone bad? On the contrary! The white substance, or "frost," found on some pods is pure vanillin and a sign of a well-aged, super-flavorful bean. The crystals should glisten, almost like sugar crystals. (If not, and if they're accompanied by a musty smell, it might be mildew and it's better to toss it.)

What's the deal with imitation vanilla? The only vanilla-related ingredient in imitation vanilla flavoring is a bit of vanillin. Other than that, you never really know what you're getting in that bottle. Most often, the remainder is lignin, a wood-pulp by-product. (Not delicious.)

Do I need to worry about the amount of alcohol in vanilla? Typically, the amount of vanilla extract relative to the total volume of a recipe is quite small. Because the majority of the extract's alcohol will evaporate during cooking, the alcohol content is not a concern for most people. But if you need to stay away from alcohol for personal, health, or religious reasons, nonalcoholic vanilla extract alternatives are available. These are easy to discern from those containing alcohol, because they're labeled "pure natural vanilla."

The FDA allows only true extracts with alcohol to be labeled "pure vanilla extract." Pure natural vanilla rarely tastes as good as extract, though, so I'd recommend using whole or ground beans instead.

What is French vanilla? French vanilla isn't a true variety of vanilla but rather a way to describe vanilla-flavored custards and ice creams that have eggs in them.

Can I grow my own vanilla? In theory, yes. But as any orchid-growing fanatic will tell you, these plants—and vanilla orchids in particular—are incredibly high maintenance. They require high heat and humidity and lots of room to grow, which is why you're much more likely to find them on a plantation near the equator than in your neighbor's backyard. Not only that, but successfully hand-pollinating, harvesting, and curing the seedpods to coax out the vanilla flavor and aroma is a whole other undertaking. Personally, I am a city girl who can't keep even a basil plant alive, so I opt to order my vanilla pods online.

What's this I hear about vanilla extract from certain places being dangerous? Vanilla extracts from places like Mexico and the Caribbean have gotten a bad rap because some temptingly cheap, inferior extracts contain chemicals banned for food use in the United States. But don't let that discourage you from trying pure, high-quality extracts made from Mexican and Caribbean beans, which are too delicious to miss. Just make sure you're always purchasing your vanilla products from reputable sources (see page 157).

ACKNOWLEDGMENTS

To have the opportunity to write another cookbook is an absolute thrill, but to work with the team that helped bring this book to life is nothing short of a dream come true. Thank you to the entire crew at Quirk Books for loving the sweet, dreamy flavor of vanilla as much as I do, and for giving this book the green light. Special thanks to my endlessly supportive editor and ad hoc therapist, Margaret McGuire.

Every cookbook author should be so lucky to shoot their books with photographer Leigh Beisch, her warm, enthusiastic crew, and the ever-inspiring art director and prop stylist Sara Slavin. Thank you all again for your support and creativity and for bringing my recipes to life. A special shout-out goes to Cathy Lopez for doing some beautiful last-minute styling for the Vanilla Cloud Cake—you saved the day!

Thank you to the awesome readers of my blog, *Piece of Cake*, and countless online friends who are always such wonderful cheerleaders and a constant source of creative fuel. Thanks to Brent Reame and the folks at Beanilla for sourcing incredible products and supplying information about them with great passion.

To my Gramma, who impresses everyone she meets with her warmth, humor, and kindness, thank you for providing me with a lifetime of love and advice and so many family recipes that have inspired my work. To my beloved friends and family, I love you all. And most of all, to my husband, Scott, and little girl Caroline: thank you for bearing the brunt of my craziness, being my ultimate taste-testers, and showing me true love—you are my heart.

BREAKFASTS

Although we most often associate vanilla flavor with desserts, beginning the day with vanilla at breakfast is a no-brainer. A splash of pure extract in a homemade granola recipe or a scraping of vanilla bean caviar into your morning oatmeal is perfect for adding a hint of sweetness without extra sugar, elevating your healthy everyday fare, and starting your day off right. But if you're anything like me, when lazy weekend mornings roll around, things like Glazed Vanilla Bean Doughnuts and rich Vanilla Bean Bread Pudding are the order of the day.

VANILLA BEAN
BREAD PUDDING

*Serves
6 to 8*

This dreamy bread pudding represents something I feel deeply about, which is to say, dessert disguised as breakfast. The amount of sugar called for is really just a suggestion; sweeten more or less according to your taste.

1 1-pound loaf rustic white bread with the crust removed from half, torn into 1-inch chunks

6 large eggs

3 cups whole milk

⅔ cup plus ¼ cup granulated sugar, divided

1 teaspoon pure vanilla extract

1 teaspoon vanilla bean paste

½ teaspoon salt

1½ teaspoons vanilla powder

• **Position a rack in the center of the oven** and preheat oven to 375°F. Butter a 2½- to 3-quart baking dish. Place bread in a large bowl. In another large bowl, whisk together eggs, milk, ⅔ cup of the sugar, vanilla extract, vanilla bean paste, and salt.

• **Pour egg mixture over bread** and stir gently to coat. Let soak for 5 to 10 minutes, or until most of the liquid is absorbed. Pour mixture into prepared baking dish.

• **In a small bowl,** whisk together the remaining ¼ cup sugar and vanilla powder. Sprinkle generously over bread mixture.

• **Bake uncovered** until bread pudding is puffed and golden and a knife inserted into the center comes out clean—from 45 to 60 minutes, depending on the size of your baking dish. Transfer dish to a wire rack and let cool for 15 minutes before serving.

Baked in individual ramekins and served with either a drizzle of White Hot Fudge (page 137) or the custard from Floating Islands (page 131), this dish makes a dynamite dinner party dessert.

½ cup dark brown sugar, packed

Caviar of 1 vanilla bean

1 teaspoon pure vanilla extract

½ teaspoon freshly ground black pepper

1 pound thick-cut applewood-smoked bacon

VANILLA, BROWN SUGAR, AND BLACK PEPPER BACON

Vanilla goes savory! This recipe is perfect for showcasing a vanilla bean with a smoky and woodsy aroma. Try heady Mexican or super-bold Tonga beans to experience the spice's savory side.

• **Position racks in the upper and lower thirds of the oven** and preheat oven to 375°F. Line 2 baking sheets with aluminum foil.

• **In a large bowl,** whisk together brown sugar, vanilla caviar, vanilla extract, and black pepper. Add bacon and toss to coat well, rubbing sugar mixture onto each slice.

• **Lay bacon strips on prepared sheets** and sprinkle any leftover sugar mixture equally over top. Bake until crisp and deeply caramelized, about 25 minutes, rotating sheets from front to back and top to bottom halfway through baking. Transfer bacon to a cooling rack set over paper towels to drain—the caramelized sugar will firm up a bit, creating a candylike glaze. Serve warm.

VANILLA BEURRE BLANC

There's not too much I can say about this silky, sexy, luxurious sauce, other than perhaps that you should put it on anything that's not nailed down. For strictly edible applications, think delicate egg dishes, sweet seafood (like lobster, shrimp, and scallops), almost any type of fish, and elegant vegetables (baby carrots, baby eggplant, and asparagus). This is pure, savory vanilla, fancy-pants-style.

⅓ cup dry white wine
3 tablespoons champagne or white wine vinegar
2 tablespoons freshly squeezed lemon juice
½ vanilla bean, split lengthwise
1 tablespoon finely minced shallots
1 cup (2 sticks) cold unsalted butter, cut into small pieces
Salt and ground white pepper, to taste

In a small saucepan, combine wine, vinegar, lemon juice, vanilla bean, and shallots. Bring to a simmer over medium-high heat and cook until reduced by half. Remove vanilla bean, scrape the caviar into the pot, and discard the pod. Reduce heat to low and begin whisking in butter, 1 small bit at a time, waiting until each is incorporated before adding the next. Season with salt and white pepper. Transfer sauce to a heatproof bowl and set over a pan of hot water to keep warm until ready to use, whisking occasionally to keep the sauce from breaking as it sits. *Makes about 1½ cups.*

 Translated from French as "white butter," this sauce is elegant yet simple to make.

1 cup steel-cut oats

½ vanilla bean, split lengthwise

2 tablespoons light brown sugar (optional), plus move for serving

¼ teaspoon ground cinnamon

⅛ teaspoon freshly grated nutmeg

⅛ teaspoon ground cardamom

Half-and-half or heavy cream, for serving

SLOW-COOKED VANILLA SPICE OATMEAL

To be frank, I am not a morning person. But if breakfast is ready and waiting before I even get out of bed, it softens the blow a bit. Slow-cooking hearty steel-cut oats requires almost no effort, and the addition of a vanilla bean transforms this humble food into something otherworldly.

• **Coat the sleeve of a 5-quart slow cooker** with nonstick cooking spray. Place sleeve in slow cooker and combine all ingredients in it; add 3½ cups water and stir to blend. Set slow cooker to low and cook for 8 hours. Remove vanilla bean and scrape any remaining caviar into oatmeal. Stir well and serve with brown sugar to taste and a drizzle of half-and-half or heavy cream (depending on the kind of day that awaits you).

Jazz up this creamy, dreamy oatmeal by increasing the water to 4 cups and adding about ⅔ cup chopped dried fruit before cooking. I love pairing dried apricots and cherries with Tahitian vanilla.

HONEY-VANILLA GRANOLA CLUSTERS

*Makes about
4 cups*

I'm a sucker for a great homemade granola. This one, with its ambrosial combination of honey and vanilla, is as good in a cereal bowl as it is eaten out of hand.

- **Position a rack in the center of the oven** and preheat oven to 325°F. Line a rimmed baking sheet with parchment paper or a silicone baking mat.

- **In a large bowl, whisk together** egg whites, brown sugar, honey, oil, and vanilla extract until smooth. Add oats and stir to coat evenly. Spread mixture onto prepared sheet in an even layer.

- **Bake for about 20 minutes,** or until golden and fragrant, stirring once or twice and rotating pan 180 degrees halfway through baking to prevent burning. Transfer baking sheet to a wire rack and let granola cool on the sheet. Break granola into clusters and store in an airtight container.

To get nice, big clusters, let the granola cool completely in one mass before breaking it into chunks.

If you like, add your favorite nuts and seeds during the last 5 minutes of baking. Try Mexican vanilla to play off the nutty, toasty flavors.

2	large egg whites, at room temperature
½	cup light brown sugar, packed
¼	cup mild clover honey
¼	cup vegetable oil
1	tablespoon pure vanilla extract
3 ½	cups old-fashioned rolled oats

Vanilla-Stewed Fruit and Honey-Vanilla Granola Custers, page 35.

VANILLA-STEWED FRUIT

*Makes about
3 cups*

Although it may sound sort of, oh, *geriatric* at first glance, this humble dish is outstanding.

• **In a medium saucepan,** stir together 2¾ cups water, orange juice, lemon juice, honey, vanilla bean, cinnamon and salt. Stir in fruit. Over medium-high heat, bring to a boil, stirring often. Reduce heat to a simmer and cook until fruit is plump and tender, 15 to 20 minutes. Using a slotted spoon, transfer fruit to a heatproof bowl. Return saucepan to high heat and boil until the liquid is reduced by half, adding any juices that drain from the fruit as it rests. Stir reduction into fruit. Serve warm, chilled, or at room temperature. Store in an airtight container in the refrigerator for up to a week.

When dried fruits are revived with fresh citrus, soft spice, and a hit of vanilla, the result is tasty and versatile: spoon it over yogurt or oatmeal (see Slow-Cooked Vanilla Spice Oatmeal, page 34) for breakfast, serve it with roasted pork or game meats, or make it into an elegant dessert over Modern Vanilla Pastry Cream (page 125), topped with a dollop of Boozy Vanilla Whipped Cream (page 127).

1 cup freshly squeezed orange juice

¼ cup freshly squeezed lemon juice

¼ cup honey

1 vanilla bean, split lengthwise

¼ teaspoon ground cinnamon

⅛ teaspoon salt

2 ounces dried apricots

2 ounces dried pears

2 ounces prunes

2 ounces dried cherries*

* *This combination of fruit is merely a guideline— use whatever dried fruits you like best.*

VANILLA-CITRUS MARINADE

One of the most remarkable things about vanilla is the way it lends roundness and a sensation of richness to a dish; the effect is similar to that of extra cream or butter. Most often, vanilla is a go-to in sweet recipes, but in the right savory applications, the results are incredible. Lighter meats, such as pork and chicken breast, and seafood like shrimp, scallops, and calamari are ideal with this surprising, flavorful marinade. It's the perfect way to experience vanilla in a whole new way, particularly if you get your hands on a more savory type of bean, such as those from India and Tonga.

⅓ cup extra-virgin olive oil
⅓ cup freshly squeezed orange juice
3 tablespoons freshly squeezed lemon juice
1 tablespoon freshly squeezed lime juice
1 clove garlic, minced
1 teaspoon orange zest
1 teaspoon lemon zest
¼ teaspoon ground white pepper
Caviar of 1 vanilla bean (pod reserved)

Whisk together ingredients in a small bowl. Pour into a large zip-top bag. Add the meat and the scraped vanilla pod. Seal the bag and gently massage the marinade into the meat. Refrigerate until ready to cook, using the following guidelines for marinating times. Remove meat from marinade and season with salt before cooking.

❋ This recipe makes about 1 cup, enough to marinate about 2 pounds of meat. Generally, I marinate pork loin or thick chops for 3 to 4 hours, chicken breasts for 2 hours, and seafood for no more than 1 hour.

VANILLA BEAN DUTCH BABY

This angelic, *wow*-inducing pancake is lovely with a simple dusting of confectioners' sugar, but you can make it truly special with a drizzle of Crème Anglaise (page 126). Either way, bring it to the table immediately, at its peak puffiness, to elicit *ooh*s and *ahh*s from your guests before you cut it.

- **Position a rack in the center of the oven** and preheat oven to 425°F. Place a 10-inch ovenproof skillet in oven to heat.

- **In a blender,** combine milk, eggs and egg white, sugar, 1 tablespoon of the butter, vanilla extract, and vanilla bean paste. Blend until smooth, about 1 minute. Add flour, baking powder, and salt and blend for 30 seconds more.

- **Remove skillet from oven.** Pour the remaining butter into the hot pan and swirl to coat evenly. Pour in batter. Bake until Dutch baby is puffed and golden, 30 to 35 minutes. Cut into quarters and serve immediately.

Viva Vanilla!

Vanilla Bean Popovers: A popover is really just a miniature Dutch baby. For smaller but equally delicious treats, pour the batter into a popover pan and bake as directed above.

⅔ cup low-fat milk*

2 large eggs, plus 1 large egg white, at room temperature

2 tablespoons granulated sugar

2 tablespoons unsalted butter, melted, divided

1 tablespoon pure vanilla extract

1 teaspoon vanilla bean paste

⅔ cup all-purpose flour

¼ teaspoon baking powder

¼ teaspoon salt

In many baking recipes, I recommend using whole milk for its great flavor, but here low-fat or even nonfat milk is best—it will yield a lighter, crisper pancake.

GLAZED VANILLA BEAN DOUGHNUTS

*Makes about
1 dozen doughnuts,
plus doughnut
holes*

**Warm fried dough. Sweet vanilla bean glaze.
I think that's all that needs to be said.**

For the doughnuts:

1 tablespoon dry active yeast

¼ cup warm water
(110°F to 115°F)

3 tablespoons granulated
sugar, divided

1 cup whole milk,
at room temperature

1 tablespoon pure
vanilla extract

Caviar of ½ vanilla bean

3 large egg yolks,
at room temperature

¼ cup (½ stick) unsalted
butter, melted and cooled

3½ cups all-purpose flour,
sifted, plus more for
kneading

1¼ teaspoons salt

Vegetable oil, for frying

• **In the bowl of a stand mixer,** whisk together yeast, warm
water, and 1 tablespoon of the sugar. Let stand until mixture is
foamy, about 5 minutes. Whisk in the remaining 2 tablespoons
sugar, milk, vanilla extract, vanilla caviar, egg yolks, and
butter. Fit the mixer with the paddle attachment and begin
mixing on low speed.

• **Add flour and salt** and mix for 3 minutes, scraping
down the sides of the bowl and the paddle often to keep
the dough moving.

• **Turn out dough** onto a lightly floured work surface and
knead by hand several times, dusting with flour as needed.
Place dough in a large oiled bowl and cover with plastic
wrap. Let rest in a warm place until doubled in bulk, about
1½ to 2 hours. (Alternatively, you can let it rise in the
refrigerator overnight, 8 to 12 hours.)

• **Turn dough out** onto a lightly floured work surface and roll
to about ½ inch thick.

**Don't let the cute little doughnut holes go
to waste! Let them rise and fry them, just like
the doughnuts.**

• **Cut out doughnuts** with a 3-inch doughnut cutter, place
on a parchment-lined baking sheet, and cover with a clean
kitchen towel. Let rise for 30 to 45 minutes, or until doughnuts
have doubled in size.

continued

GLAZED VANILLA BEAN DOUGHNUTS, CONT.

For the glaze:

1½ cups confectioners' sugar

2 tablespoons whole milk

Pinch salt

Caviar of ½ vanilla bean

• **Pour 2½ inches of vegetable oil** into a 4- or 5-quart pot and heat it to 350°F. Fry doughnuts in batches of no more than 4 until they are deep golden brown, 2 minutes per side, turning only once (turning too often can result in greasy doughnuts). Transfer to paper towels to drain.

• **For the glaze,** whisk together the confectioners' sugar, milk, salt, and vanilla caviar until smooth. Spoon glaze over warm doughnuts and serve.

Viva Vanilla!

Boston Cream Doughnuts: When cutting the doughnuts, don't cut holes from the centers (use a 3-inch circle cutter rather than a doughnut cutter). After doughnuts have cooled completely, fill with a batch of Modern Vanilla Pastry Cream (page 125): Load pastry cream into a piping bag fitted with a large round tip. Poke a hole in the side of each doughnut with a long skewer or thin knife and wiggle it around to create a hollow, being careful not to pierce the opposite side of the doughnut. Insert tip of piping bag into doughnut and fill slowly, just enough to feel the weight of the pastry cream inside. Next, make a rich chocolate glaze: Combine ½ cup heavy cream and 4 ounces bittersweet chocolate in a heatproof bowl. Microwave in 30-second bursts on high power until melted, stirring well after each interval. Stir in ½ teaspoon pure vanilla extract. Spoon the glaze over the filled doughnuts.

VANILLA BEAN HONEY BUTTER

There's nothing better on a hot, freshly baked scone or muffin than a dab of butter. But when you combine the sweet flavors of vanilla and honey with it, ooh…that's some next-level stuff, right there. Lush, creamy European-style butter turns this simple spread into a luxurious treat.

I like to use vanilla bean paste for convenience, but if you happen to get your hands on a specialty honey with vibrant fruity or floral notes, a scraped Tahitian bean is a wonderful accompaniment.

4 ounces European-style butter (such as Plugrá), at room temperature
2 teaspoons vanilla bean paste
2 tablespoons honey
$\frac{1}{8}$ teaspoon salt

In the bowl of an electric mixer fitted with the paddle attachment, beat together ingredients until smooth and creamy, scraping down sides of bowl often. Serve immediately or pack into a ramekin or small wide-mouth jar, cover with plastic wrap, and store in the refrigerator. Let honey butter soften to room temperature before serving. *Makes about ½ cup*

❋ This butter is a dream when spread on Light, Crisp Vanilla Waffles (page 45) or Vanilla Bean Popovers (page 39).

LIGHT, CRISP VANILLA WAFFLES

Makes 8
7-inch round
waffles

In my lifelong quest for a perfectly light, crisp waffle, I learned early on that I wouldn't get the desired results with a dump-and-stir recipe. This recipe requires a little extra fuss, but the ethereal texture is totally worth it.

• **Preheat a waffle iron** to medium-high heat.

• **Sift together** flour, sugar, baking powder, baking soda, and salt into a large bowl.

• **In a medium bowl,** whisk together buttermilk, egg yolk, vanilla extract, vanilla bean paste or caviar, and oil until smooth. Whisk in club soda. Gently whisk the wet ingredients into the dry ingredients just until smooth.

• **In a small clean bowl with clean beaters,** beat egg whites until they hold firm peaks. Gently fold into the batter until well blended. Pour batter onto waffle iron and cook until deeply golden. Serve waffles immediately.

The longer the waffles cook, the crisper they will be. If you notice a few pale spots, let them continue to cook until they're evenly browned all over.

1 cup all-purpose flour

1 tablespoon granulated sugar

1 teaspoon baking powder

¼ teaspoon baking soda

¼ teaspoon salt

½ cup buttermilk

1 large egg yolk

1 tablespoon pure vanilla extract

1 teaspoon vanilla bean paste

3 tablespoons vegetable oil

½ cup club soda

2 large egg whites

VANILLA-BOURBON MAPLE SYRUP

Even though Madagascar Bourbon vanilla has nothing to do with liquor, you wouldn't know it from the magical way vanilla pairs with that dark, heady booze. Something really special happens when you combine these two rich, complex flavors with pure maple syrup. It elevates breakfast to a whole new level.

Pour ½ cup bourbon into a small saucepan. Add 2 vanilla beans, split lengthwise. Bring to a boil over high heat and continue boiling until bourbon is reduced by half. Stir in 1½ cups pure maple syrup (I like dark grade A amber) and a pinch of salt. Remove the pod and scrape the caviar into the syrup or, if you like, leave the pods in the syrup so the vanilla flavor intensifies over time. *Makes about 1¾ cups*

❋ Keep a jar of Vanilla-Bourbon Maple Syrup in your kitchen, and you'll be prepared to make any brunch special. Or add a label and a ribbon bow for giving to friends.

BUTTERY BAKED VANILLA BEAN FRENCH TOAST

This decadent make-ahead wonder is a riff on a recipe from one of my best friends. Her mom adds bits of chopped apple and some cinnamon in the mix, and to make things extra Midwestern, a bit more butter and sugar. It's divine. This formula is lighter and a touch fancier, calling for brioche or challah instead of plain white bread and a sprinkling of toasty almonds and fragrant vanilla sugar on top.

• **In a small bowl,** combine the raisins with ½ cup hot water. Let soak for about 30 minutes.

• **Brush 1 tablespoon of melted butter** over the bottom and sides of a 9-by-13-inch baking dish. Drain raisins and pat dry; scatter them in an even layer in the bottom of baking dish.

• **In a blender,** combine the remaining 5 tablespoons melted butter with milk, eggs, brown sugar, vanilla bean paste, and salt. Blend on high speed until smooth, about 1 minute. Arrange bread slices in baking dish, trimming them as needed so that no gaps remain. Pour batter evenly over top. Cover dish with aluminum foil and let soak at least 4 hours or overnight.

• **To bake,** position a rack in the center of the oven and preheat the oven to 375°F. In a small bowl, use your fingers to toss together almonds, vanilla sugar, and about 1 teaspoon water—just enough to moisten the mixture. Scatter topping evenly over the soaked bread. Re-cover dish with foil and bake for 40 minutes, then remove foil and continue baking until bread is slightly puffed and lightly browned on top, 10 to 15 minutes more. Let cool for 10 minutes before serving.

For the French toast:

½ cup golden raisins*

6 tablespoons unsalted butter, melted and cooled, divided

1½ cups whole milk

6 large eggs

¾ cup light brown sugar, packed

1 tablespoon vanilla bean paste

¼ teaspoon salt

1 1-pound loaf brioche or challah, cut into 1½-inch-thick slices

For the topping:

¾ cup sliced almonds

¼ cup Vanilla Sugar (page 69), or ¼ cup granulated sugar plus 1½ teaspoons vanilla powder

* *Soak the raisins in hot water, as directed, or in vanilla-infused liquor (page 151), for a little extra kick first thing in the morning.*

CAKES & PIES

Vanilla versions of cakes and pies are classic. Perfect for pairing with just about any frosting, topping, or filling, they're like a backdrop of inspiration just waiting to be jazzed up. But here, pure vanilla flavor *is* the jazzy part. Some recipes in this chapter are modernized versions of beloved family recipes I've eaten my entire life. Others are my take on classic cakes and pies, with the vanilla flavor amped way up—the show-stopping Vanilla Cloud Cake will make even the most ardent chocolate cake lovers doubt their dedication. All are timeless, versatile, and ultimate crowd-pleasers.

ULTIMATE VANILLA CUPCAKES

Makes
15 frosted
cupcakes

Ah, the cupcake. It may be ubiquitous nowadays, but who doesn't feel happy when faced with a sweet, adorable, individually portioned treat? This pairing of light (but not preciously so) cake and creamy, not-too-sweet frosting strikes a perfect balance of tastes and textures.

• **Position racks in the upper and lower thirds of the oven** and preheat oven to 350°F. Line 15 wells of two 12-cup muffin tins with paper liners. Lightly brush vegetable oil around the edges of the wells (in case cupcakes rise over the liners).

• **Sift together** flours, baking powder, and salt into a medium bowl.

• **In the bowl of a stand mixer** fitted with the paddle attachment, beat together butter, sugar, vanilla extract, and vanilla bean paste or caviar until light and fluffy, about 2 minutes.

• **In a large measuring cup** (for easy pouring), whisk together sour cream, eggs, and egg yolk until smooth. With the mixer running on medium-low speed, pour about half of the wet ingredients into the butter-sugar mixture, beating until smooth. Reduce mixer speed to low and stir in half of the flour mixture. Add half of the remaining wet ingredients and mix until smooth. Repeat with remaining dry and wet ingredients. Turn off mixer and fold batter by hand several times to make sure it is well mixed.

continued

For the cupcakes:

- ½ cup plus 2 tablespoons cake flour
- ½ cup all-purpose flour
- 1½ teaspoons baking powder
- ¼ teaspoon salt
- ½ cup (1 stick) unsalted butter, cut into tablespoons, at room temperature
- 1 cup granulated sugar
- 1½ teaspoons pure vanilla extract
- ½ teaspoon vanilla bean paste
- ½ cup sour cream
- 2 large eggs plus 1 large egg yolk

For the frosting:

2 cups confectioners' sugar, sifted

1 tablespoon plus 1 teaspoon milk

1 teaspoon pure vanilla extract

$\frac{1}{8}$ teaspoon salt

14 tablespoons ($1\frac{3}{4}$ sticks) unsalted butter, cut into tablespoons, at cool room temperature*

1 teaspoon vanilla bean paste, or caviar of $\frac{1}{2}$ vanilla bean

For a smooth and sturdy frosting, don't let the butter get too warm before working with it. It should give when you press your finger into it but still be cool to the touch and almost waxy in texture. If it looks shiny, it's too warm; chill it a bit before using.

• **Fill muffin cups** no more than two-thirds full of batter. Bake until cupcakes are golden and a toothpick inserted into the center comes out clean, 22 to 25 minutes; rotate pans from top to bottom and front to back halfway through baking. Let cupcakes cool in the pans for 5 minutes, then remove from pan and let cool completely on a wire rack.

• **To make the frosting,** place confectioners' sugar in the bowl of a stand mixer fitted with the paddle attachment. Add milk, vanilla extract, and salt and mix on low speed until sugar is evenly moistened (it will still look quite dry). Add butter and gradually increase the speed from low to medium-high. Beat until fluffy and light in texture, 3 to 4 minutes. Beat in the vanilla bean paste or caviar during the last minute. Frost the cooled cupcakes liberally.

This recipe makes enough frosting to top each cupcake with a generous ½-inch layer. To create the dramatic frosting clouds seen in the photo, double the frosting recipe. Load the frosting into a piping bag fitted with a large round tip, and pipe the frosting in concentric circles.

VANILLA CLOUD CAKE

Oh. *This cake.* **Every time I serve it or share the recipe, I am told it is the best cake the person has ever had. It truly is something special and lives up to its ethereal name, with a serious punch of vanilla flavor. Have an empty wine bottle or similar vessel at the ready for inverting the cake during the cooling process—you want the pan to be high above the countertop so air can circulate all around as the cake cools.**

- **Position a rack in the lower third of the oven** and preheat oven to 350°F. Sift together half of the sugar and flour into a medium bowl.

- **In the bowl of a stand mixer** fitted with the whisk attachment, beat egg whites, cream of tartar, and salt on medium-high speed until mixture holds soft peaks, 2 to 3 minutes. With the mixer still running, slowly pour in the remaining sugar and beat until mixture is glossy and holds stiff peaks. Beat in vanilla bean paste.

- **Sift flour mixture** in three additions into egg-white mixture, gently folding after each addition to incorporate. Scrape batter into a 10-inch angel food cake pan with a removable bottom and smooth the top with a spatula. Bake for 40 to 45 minutes, or until cake is deeply golden with a deep cracks in the surface and a toothpick inserted into the center comes out with just a few moist crumbs (a metal tester will come out clean even if cake is not done). Invert the pan onto the bottle

continued

For the cake:

- 1½ cups superfine sugar, divided*
- ¾ cup cake flour
- 2 cups egg whites (about 16 large egg whites), at room temperature
- 2 teaspoons cream of tartar
- ½ teaspoon salt
- 1 tablespoon vanilla bean paste

* *Make superfine sugar by grinding granulated sugar in a food processor or clean coffee grinder.*

VANILLA CLOUD
CAKE, CONT.

and let cool completely. Run a thin spatula along the sides and around the center of the cake to loosen from pan and transfer to a serving platter.

• **To make the frosting,** beat together cream cheese and white chocolate in the bowl of a stand mixer until smooth and creamy. In a separate bowl, whip together cream, vanilla extract, and vanilla bean paste until stiff peaks form. Gently stir about one-third of the whipped cream into the cream cheese mixture to lighten it, then gently fold in the remaining whipped cream.

• **Frost the cake generously,** using the back of a tablespoon to create swoops and swirls.

For the frosting:

8 ounces cream cheese, at room temperature

6 ounces white chocolate, melted and cooled

2 cups heavy cream, very cold

1 tablespoon pure vanilla extract

1 teaspoon vanilla bean paste

For the cake:

1½ cups cake flour

⅛ teaspoon salt

⅛ teaspoon baking soda

½ cup (1 stick) unsalted butter, at room temperature

1¼ cups Vanilla Sugar (page 69)

1½ teaspoons pure vanilla extract

Caviar of ½ vanilla bean

3 large eggs, at room temperature

½ cup buttermilk, at room temperature

TRIPLE VANILLA POUND CAKE

This is a family heirloom recipe turned vanilla triple threat. With vanilla sugar, caviar, and extract, there's a breath of vanilla in every bite. Double-glazing makes for an insanely moist, tender cake with an irresistible sugary crisp exterior.

• **Position a rack in the center of the oven** and preheat oven to 325°F. Spray a 9-by-5-inch loaf pan with nonstick cooking spray and line it with parchment paper.

• **Sift together** flour, salt, and baking soda into a medium bowl.

• **In the bowl of a stand mixer** fitted with the paddle attachment, beat together butter, vanilla sugar, vanilla extract, and vanilla caviar on medium-high speed until light and fluffy, about 2 minutes. Beat in eggs, 1 at a time, until smooth. Reduce mixer speed to low and add buttermilk. Gradually add flour mixture. Turn off mixer and finish stirring batter by hand until well mixed. Scrape batter into prepared pan.

• **Bake until a toothpick inserted** in the center comes out clean, 60 to 70 minutes. Set pan on a wire rack to cool for 20 minutes.

• **While cake cools, make the glaze:** Whisk together sugar, vanilla caviar, and buttermilk. Whisk in butter until smooth. Set a wire rack over a large baking sheet covered with foil or parchment paper for easy cleanup. Remove the cake (it should be cool enough to handle, but still warm) from the pan and set on the wire rack.

• **Slowly pour glaze over cake,** using an offset spatula to smooth and spread it over the top and along the sides as your pour. Let set for 10 minutes. Remove rack from sheet pan and, with a spoon or spatula, scrape up the excess glaze and put it back in the bowl. Place rack over sheet pan again and glaze cake a second time. Let stand at least 1 hour, until cake has cooled completely and glaze has set, before slicing and serving.

For the glaze:

1½ cups confectioners' sugar

Caviar of ½ vanilla bean

2 to 3 tablespoons buttermilk, at room temperature

1 tablespoon unsalted butter, very soft

For the crust:

1 batch Vanilla Snaps
 (page 80), or 8 ounces
 store-bought vanilla wafers
 (about 50 wafers)

6 tablespoons unsalted butter,
 melted

1 tablespoon granulated sugar

½ teaspoon pure vanilla extract

¼ teaspoon salt

For the filling:

3 pounds (6 8-ounce packages)
 cream cheese, at room
 temperature

1½ cups granulated sugar

5 large eggs

2 tablespoons freshly squeezed
 lemon juice

1 tablespoon pure
 vanilla extract

1 tablespoon vanilla
 bean paste

BIG MAMA VANILLA CHEESECAKE

If you're looking for a show-stopping cheesecake recipe, look no further. This one features a sweet and salty crust made with vanilla wafers rather than predictable graham crackers.

• **Position a rack in the center of the oven** and preheat oven to 325°F. Lightly spray the sides of a 10-inch springform pan with nonstick cooking spray (no need to spray the bottom).

• **In the bowl of a food processor,** process vanilla wafers to fine crumbs. Add butter, sugar, vanilla extract, and salt and pulse until well mixed and evenly moistened. Pour mixture into prepared pan and press firmly along the bottom and about 2 inches up the sides of pan.

• **Next, make the filling:** In the bowl of a stand mixer fitted with the paddle attachment, beat cream cheese until soft and smooth. Add sugar and beat until fluffy.

• **Beat in eggs 1 at a time.** Turn off mixer and thoroughly scrape down the sides and bottom of the bowl. Add lemon juice, vanilla extract, and vanilla bean paste and beat 1 minute more. Pour batter into prepared pan. Bake until filling is set around the edges but still jiggles slightly in the center, 50 to 60 minutes. Place plan on a wire rack to cool for 10 minutes. Leave oven on.

• **For the topping,** whisk together sour cream, sugar, lemon juice, and vanilla extract in a medium bowl. Pour over cheesecake and spread with a spatula to completely cover the surface. Return pan to oven to bake for 8 to 10 minutes more, until topping is slightly firm but hasn't taken on any color.

• **Return pan to wire rack** and let cheesecake cool to room temperature. Refrigerate for at least 6 hours, until cheesecake is set, before removing from pan and serving.

This beauty must chill in the refrigerator for at least 6 hours before serving, but boy is it worth it. If you're looking for something fast, try the Quick Vanilla Bean Cheesecake (page 63).

For the topping:

2 cups sour cream

1/3 cup granulated sugar

1 tablespoon freshly squeezed lemon juice

2 teaspoons pure vanilla extract

TWINKIE BUNDT CAKE

This cake is essentially an enormous from-scratch version of the iconic American snack cake, with the vanilla flavor amplified and made with pronounceable ingredients. It's golden and terrifically moist, and its cream-filled cross-section is an instant joy-inducer.

• **Position a rack in the lower third of the oven** and preheat oven to 325°F. Coat a 12-cup Bundt pan with nonstick cooking spray and dust it lightly with flour.

• **Sift together** flour, baking powder, and salt into a large bowl.

• **In the bowl of a stand mixer** fitted with the paddle attachment, beat butter and vanilla extract on medium speed until smooth and creamy. Add sugar and beat until evenly mixed, about 1 minute. Slowly pour in oil. Beat until light and fluffy, about 2 minutes. Add eggs and egg yolks, 1 at a time, beating thoroughly after each addition.

• **Reduce mixer speed to low.** Stir in flour mixture and buttermilk in three alternating additions, ending with the buttermilk, and continue to mix on low speed until batter is smooth and no lumps remain. Turn off mixer and fold batter several times by hand to ensure everything is well incorporated, and then pour batter into prepared pan.

continued

For the cake:

3 cups cake flour

1 tablespoon baking powder

¾ teaspoon salt

6 tablespoons unsalted butter, at room temperature

1 tablespoon pure vanilla extract

2 cups granulated sugar

½ cup vegetable oil

3 large eggs plus 4 large egg yolks, at room temperature

1 cup buttermilk, at room temperature

TWINKIE BUNDT CAKE, CONT.

For the cream filling:

1 (7.5-ounce) jar marshmallow crème

½ cup (1 stick) unsalted butter, at room temperature

1 teaspoon pure vanilla extract

Confectioners' sugar, for dusting (optional)

• **Bake for 60 to 70 minutes,** until the cake is golden, the top springs back when lightly pressed, and a cake tester inserted into the center comes out clean. Place pan on a wire rack and let cool completely, about 2 hours.

• **For the filling,** in the bowl of a stand mixer, beat together marshmallow crème and butter until smooth. Transfer to a pastry bag fitted with a large round tip.

• **With the cake still in the pan,** use a paring knife or an apple corer to cut 6 or 7 deep holes into bottom of cake, each about ¾ inch in diameter; be careful not to cut through top of cake. Discard (i.e., nibble) cake scraps. With your fingers, gently burrow a horizontal tunnel around the center of the cake, connecting the vertical holes.

• **Insert the tip of the pastry bag** into each hole and squeeze in filling, tilting pastry bag back and forth as you work to encourage filling into the horizontal tunnel through the cake. When cake is filled, use a spatula to scrape away excess filling from the bottom of the cake. Quickly and carefully invert cake onto a serving platter. Dust with confectioners' sugar, if desired, and serve.

QUICK VANILLA BEAN CHEESECAKE

*Serves
8 to 10*

My mom never did much baking, but there were a couple of recipes she would bust out from time to time. This kitschy, crustless (!), and completely addictive cheesecake was one of them. It's my earliest memory of dessert—which is saying a lot, given my sweet tooth—and a perennial favorite.

• **Position a rack in the center of the oven** and preheat oven to 350°F. Coat a 9-inch ceramic or glass pie plate with nonstick cooking spray.

• **In a large bowl,** place cream cheese, eggs, vanilla bean paste, lemon juice, ¾ cup of the sugar, and baking mix. Mix with an electric mixer on low speed until incorporated, then increase speed to medium-high and beat for 3 minutes, scraping down the sides and bottom of the bowl as necessary.

• **Pour into prepared baking dish** and bake for 45 to 50 minute, until cheesecake is slightly puffed and golden brown on top and a toothpick inserted in the center comes out clean. Let cool on a wire rack; cake will deflate a bit as it cools.

• **To make the sour-cream topping,** stir together sour cream, the remaining 2 tablespoons sugar, and vanilla extract until well blended.

• **Pour topping over cheesecake** and smooth with a small spatula. Refrigerate until chilled and set, at least 2 hours, before serving. Cover any leftovers tightly with plastic wrap and store in the refrigerator for up to 4 days.

For the cheesecake:

2 8-ounce packages cream cheese,* at room temperature

2 large eggs, at room temperature

2 teaspoons vanilla bean paste

1 tablespoon plus 1 teaspoon freshly squeezed lemon juice

¾ cup plus 2 tablespoons granulated sugar, divided

¼ cup all-purpose baking mix (such as Bisquick)

8 ounces sour cream

2 teaspoons pure vanilla extract

* *I recommend Philadelphia brand for cheesecakes.*

TRES LECHES CAKE

If ever there was a cake to make the masses forget about chocolate forever, this decadent, milky, vanilla-soaked number just might be it. You can embellish it several ways: with edible flowers, fresh summer berries, or, for a retro take for the holidays, maraschino cherries. But I think that a big bowl, a big spoon, and a comfy couch are the best serving suggestion of all.

For the cake:

1 cup all-purpose flour

1½ teaspoons baking powder

¼ teaspoon salt

⅓ cup whole milk

2 teaspoons pure
   vanilla extract

5 large eggs, separated,
   at room temperature

1 cup granulated sugar,
   divided

For soaking the cake:

1¼ cups evaporated milk

1 cup sweetened
   condensed milk

¼ cup heavy cream

• **Position a rack in the center of the oven** and preheat oven to 350°F. Coat a 10-inch springform pan with nonstick cooking spray.

• **Sift together** flour, baking powder, and salt into a medium bowl. Microwave milk on high power for 1 minute. Stir in vanilla extract.

• **In the bowl of an electric mixer** fitted with the paddle attachment, beat egg yolks and ¾ cup of the sugar until light in color and doubled in volume, about 3 minutes. Reduce mixer speed to low and stir in the milk mixture.

• **Gradually stir in the flour mixture;** when just a few streaks of flour remain, turn off mixer and stir batter gently by hand until well blended. Set aside.

• **In a clean bowl with clean beaters,** beat egg whites on medium-high speed until they hold soft peaks, 2 to 3 minutes. Gradually add the remaining ¼ cup sugar. Beat until mixture holds stiff, glossy peaks, about 1 minute more.

• **Fold one-third** of the egg-white mixture into the batter, to lighten it. Gently fold in the remaining egg-white mixture. Pour batter into prepared pan and smooth the top with a spatula.

• **Bake until cake is a deep golden brown** and a cake tester inserted into the center comes out clean, 45 to 50 minutes. Transfer pan to a wire rack to cool completely, at least 1 hour. (The cake will probably sink a bit during cooling, but don't worry.)

• **Place cooled cake** in a deep serving platter or wide, shallow bowl. Pierce all over the top and sides with a bamboo skewer or fork.

• **In a medium bowl,** whisk together evaporated milk, sweetened condensed milk, and cream. Slowly pour mixture over cake, swirling around cake and lifting the edges to ensure the liquid is fully absorbed underneath and on all sides.

• **For the topping,** place cream, vanilla extract, and vanilla bean paste in a clean bowl. With clean beaters, whip until mixture holds firm peaks. Cover cake with swirls of whipped cream. Serve immediately.

Though this recipe won't fully use up standard cans of evaporated and sweetened condensed milks, the combined remainder is dynamite in coffee. See page 123 for how to make Homemade Vanilla Coffee Creamer.

For the topping:

1¾ cups heavy cream

1 teaspoon pure vanilla extract

1 teaspoon vanilla bean paste

CHERRY-VANILLA SHORTBREAD CAKE SQUARES

*Makes
2 dozen 3-inch
squares*

Like my **Quick Vanilla Bean Cheesecake (page 63),** this recipe is an updated version of a childhood favorite. I thought long and hard about forgoing the canned cherry pie filling in favor of homemade cherry compote, but ultimately I gave in to tradition. I adore that this simple, homey dessert has all the kitsch and charm of an old Midwestern lady's recipe box. Plus, there are some tasty, high-quality commercial pie fillings available these days.

1 cup (2 sticks) unsalted butter, at room temperature

1½ cups granulated sugar

1 tablespoon freshly squeezed lemon juice

1 tablespoon pure vanilla extract

½ teaspoon salt

4 large eggs, at room temperature

2 cups all-purpose flour

1 21-ounce can cherry pie filling

1 teaspoon vanilla bean paste

Confectioners' sugar, for dusting

• **Position a rack in the center of the oven** and preheat oven to 350°F. Coat a 12-by-17-by-1-inch rimmed baking sheet with cooking spray, line it with parchment paper, and lightly spray the parchment, too.

• **In the bowl of a stand mixer,** beat together butter and sugar until very light and fluffy, about 2 minutes. Beat in lemon juice, vanilla extract, and salt. Beat in eggs 1 at a time. Scrape down the sides of the bowl. Turn mixer to the lowest speed and stir in flour. To avoid overbeating, stop mixing when a few streaks of flour remain in the batter; stir by hand until no flour remains.

• **Scrape batter into prepared pan** and smooth it into an even layer. Score it into 24 squares with a toothpick. (Don't worry about making the squares perfectly even—the lines will disappear during baking. This step is to make placing the cherries easier.)

continued

CHERRY-VANILLA SHORTBREAD CAKE SQUARES, CONT.

• **In a small bowl,** stir together pie filling and vanilla bean paste. Place 3 cherries in the center of each square. Bake shortbread until a toothpick inserted into the center comes out clean, about 30 minutes. Transfer pan to a wire rack to cool completely. Just before serving, cut shortbread into 24 squares and dust with powdered sugar.

Store leftovers in an airtight container between layers of waxed paper or parchment; squares will keep for up to 3 days.

HOMEMADE VANILLA SUGAR

If you're anything like me, the elegant canisters of vanilla sugar sold in gourmet shops and grocery stores tempt you with their dreaminess…until you see the eye-popping price tag. I'll let you in on a little secret: you can totally make your own, and for dirt cheap. Here's how:

Fill a lidded container with about 2 cups granulated sugar. Bury a vanilla bean (or two, for more intense flavor), split lengthwise, in the sugar. Tighten the lid and shake the container like you're competing in a dance contest at a dive bar. Store in a cool, dark place for 2 days and then open the container, take a deep whiff, and die a little from the glorious fragrance of homemade vanilla sugar. It's that easy! You don't even need a whole unscraped pod—use the empty scraped vanilla beans from recipes that call for just the caviar. Store the empty pods in the sugar; when your supply runs low, replenish by adding more fresh sugar on top.

Use vanilla sugar the same way you use the granulated stuff. It adds a bit more oomph to baked goods and is a delicious addition to coffee and tea. If you're making vanilla-forward recipes like the ones in this book, vanilla sugar is yet another simple way to add that irresistibly ambrosial flavor.

To turn this recipe into a gift, pack the vanilla sugar in a decorative container—like a vintage Mason jar—topped with a scrap of fabric and festive ribbon. For an even fancier version, use raw turbinado sugar instead of granulated sugar.

❋ As a general rule, you'll want to use about 2 cups of sugar per bean.

VANILLA CREAM PIE

*Makes 1
9-inch pie*

**All-American and unassuming, vanilla cream pie
is a diner staple and a totally satisfying end to a
meal. I think even a mediocre vanilla cream pie
is still pretty dang good. Here I set out to make
something irresistible, with vanilla singing in
the salty-sweet crust, the creamy filling, *and* the
mound of whipped cream on top.**

• **Position a rack in the center of the oven** and preheat
oven to 350°F.

• **In the bowl of a food processor,** process vanilla wafers to
fine crumbs. Add butter, sugar, vanilla extract, and salt and
pulse until ingredients are well mixed and evenly moistened.
Press mixture firmly along the bottom and up the sides of a
9-inch metal or glass pie plate. Bake until lightly golden and
fragrant, 10 to 12 minutes. Transfer pan to a wire rack and let
crust cool completely, about 45 minutes.

• **Pour pastry cream** into the cooled crust. Cover with
plastic wrap and refrigerate until filling is cold and set, at
least 4 hours.

• **Immediately before serving,** whip heavy cream, sugar,
and vanilla extract in a medium bowl with an electric mixer
until mixture holds firm peaks. Top pie with swirls of whipped
cream. This pie is best eaten the day it's made.

For the crust:

8 ounces store-bought vanilla
wafers, or 8 ounces Vanilla
Snaps (page 80)

6 tablespoons unsalted butter,
melted and cooled

1 tablespoon granulated sugar

½ teaspoon pure
vanilla extract

¼ teaspoon salt

For the filling and topping:

1 batch Modern Vanilla Pastry
Cream (page 125), made with 5
tablespoons cornstarch*

1¾ cups heavy cream, chilled

1 tablespoon granulated sugar

1 teaspoon pure vanilla extract

* *Increase the cornstarch in the
pastry cream to 5 tablespoons
and prepare as instructed on
page 125.*

Serves
6 to 8

For the meringue shell:

1 batch Vanilla Bean Meringue
  Kisses batter (page 91)

For the topping:

2 tablespoons granulated sugar

2 teaspoons cornstarch

1 tablespoon freshly squeezed
  lemon juice

12 ounces frozen blueberries,
  slightly thawed*

½ teaspoon pure
  vanilla extract**

** Blueberries are only one option.
Try different frozen berries,
dark sweet cherries, or chopped
stone fruits like peaches.*

*** I like using Tahitian vanilla in
this recipe; it's a perfect
complement to cream and fruits
of all sorts.*

VANILLA MASCARPONE PAVLOVA

For my last meal on earth, I'd request a pavlova for dessert: a light, crisp meringue disk with a marshmallowy center, piled high with whipped cream and juicy fruit. It's a party of flavors and textures—and just about the most perfect dessert ever created. This recipe is packed with irresistible vanilla every step of the way. It's made even more luxurious thanks to the mascarpone cheese in the cream topping.

• **Position a rack in the center of the oven** and preheat oven to 225°F. Line a large baking sheet with parchment paper or a silicone baking mat.

• **Rather than piping the meringue** into cookies as on page 91, transfer it from the mixer bowl to the center of the prepared baking sheet. Use an offset spatula to shape the meringue into a disk about 9 inches in diameter. Bake until dry and firm to the touch, about 1½ hours. Turn off oven, crack open the door, and let meringue cool completely in oven, about 1 hour more.

• **For the topping,** whisk together ¼ cup water, sugar, cornstarch, and lemon juice in a medium saucepan. Add blueberries and stir to combine. Cook over medium heat, stirring often. Boil for 2 minutes. Remove pan from heat and stir in vanilla extract. Transfer to a medium bowl and refrigerate, stirring occasionally, until completely cool, about 1 hour.

• **In a clean mixer bowl** with clean beaters, beat together mascarpone cheese, sugar, vanilla bean paste, and vanilla extract. In a separate bowl, beat cream to stiff peaks. Gently fold about one-third of the whipped cream into the mascarpone mixture to lighten it, then gently fold in remaining cream.

• **When you're ready to assemble** the pavlova, set meringue shell on a serving platter or cake stand. Pile it high with vanilla mascarpone cream, spreading it into an even layer. Pour fruit topping over the top. Serve immediately.

Anytime you have a hankering for meringue-making, first check the weather report: dry, cool days are best. Humidity can prevent the meringue from drying and crisping properly.

For the vanilla mascarpone cream:

6 ounces mascarpone cheese, at room temperature

¼ cup granulated sugar

2 teaspoons vanilla bean paste

1 teaspoon pure vanilla extract

¾ cup heavy cream, chilled

COOKIES & BARS

Of all the hundreds (thousands, millions!) of cookie recipes, you'd be hard-pressed to find many that don't contain vanilla extract. After all, vanilla's complex notes are perfect for heightening so many other, bolder flavors in cookies—chocolate, fruits, nuts, spices, booze. But featuring vanilla as the star flavor can be a challenge: the small surface area of cookies and the high heat required to bake them often cause the vanilla flavor to bake off. For cookies with big vanilla impact, pull out the big guns—premium extracts and bean pastes—and use both in a single recipe. And sandwiching a creamy vanilla bean filling between those cookies doesn't hurt, either.

BIG, SOFT FROSTED VANILLA SUGAR COOKIES

Makes 18 4-inch frosted cookies

This recipe was inspired by the mass-produced, cakey frosted cookies from the supermarket that are a favorite of my husband but also full of unpronounceable ingredients. If you think those technicolor gems are good, be prepared to be blown away by this from-scratch version.

• **Sift flour, salt, and baking powder** together into a medium bowl. In the bowl of a stand mixer fitted with the paddle attachment, beat butter and vanilla extract until creamy. Add sugar and beat on medium-high speed until light and fluffy, about 2 minutes.

• **In a small bowl,** whisk together oil, eggs, and corn syrup until well blended. Reduce mixer speed to medium-low and beat egg mixture into butter mixture until smooth, light, and fluffy. Reduce mixer speed to low and gradually stir in flour mixture until evenly mixed. Cover bowl with plastic wrap and refrigerate until firm, at least 2 hours.

• **When you're ready to bake,** position racks in the upper and lower thirds of the oven and preheat oven to 325°F. Line 2 baking sheets with parchment paper or silicone baking mats.

• **Using a standard ice-cream scoop** or two large spoons, drop dough in ¼-cup scoops onto baking sheets, 3 per sheet. (You will need to bake cookies in 3 batches.) Bake until

For the cookies:

- 3½ cups cake flour
- ½ teaspoon salt
- 1 teaspoon baking powder
- 1 cup (2 sticks) unsalted butter, at room temperature
- 2 tablespoons pure vanilla extract
- 1⅓ cups granulated sugar
- ½ cup vegetable oil
- 2 large eggs, at room temperature
- 2 tablespoons light corn syrup

continued

BIG, SOFT FROSTED VANILLA SUGAR COOKIES, CONT.

For the frosting:

1 cup (2 sticks) unsalted butter, at room temperature

4 cups confectioners' sugar, sifted

¼ cup milk

⅛ teaspoon salt

2 teaspoons vanilla bean paste

1 teaspoon pure vanilla extract

cookies are just turning pale golden around the edges, about 15 to 17 minutes, rotating sheets from front to back and top to bottom halfway through baking. Do not overbake. Let cookies cool on baking sheets for at least 10 minutes, then transfer to a cooling rack. Repeat with the remaining dough.

• **To make the frosting,** place all ingredients in the bowl of a stand mixer fitted with the paddle attachment. Begin beating on low speed and gradually increase the speed to medium. Beat until frosting is smooth and creamy, about 1 minute. Frost cooled cookies generously.

This recipe makes gloriously large cookies, like the ones sold at coffeeshops. If you want smaller cookies, scoop them into 2-tablespoon-size portions, 6 per baking sheet. The baking temperature and time are the same.

Viva Vanilla!

Vanilla Latte Cookies: Whisk 1½ teaspoons instant espresso powder into the dry ingredients and beat another ½ teaspoon into the frosting.

VANILLA BEAN TUILES

Vanilla's flavor seems to pair well with just about every texture of sweet treat you can imagine. Crisp, creamy, brittle, cakey, gooey—you name it, vanilla complements it. One of my favorite ways to add complexity to an all-vanilla dessert is to combine multiple textures rather than different flavors. These light, crisp vanilla tuiles can elevate a simple, homey dessert just by adding a bit of crunch. Serve a few with a dish of Favorite Vanilla Ice Cream (page 135)—your guests won't even think about chocolate.

 2 large egg whites
 6 tablespoons granulated sugar
 5 tablespoons melted butter
 1 teaspoon vanilla bean paste
 $\frac{1}{8}$ teaspoon salt
 $\frac{1}{3}$ cup all-purpose flour

To make these super-simple cookies, preheat the oven to 350°F. Line a baking sheet with a silicone baking mat. In a large bowl, whisk together egg whites, sugar, butter, vanilla bean paste, and salt until smooth. Add flour and whisk to blend well.

Scoop batter onto prepared sheet in 2-teaspoon dollops. Use a small offset spatula or your fingertip to smooth into thin 3-inch rounds, spaced 1 inch apart. Bake until cookies are lightly golden all over and deeply golden at the edges, about 8 to 9 minutes. Using an offset spatula, carefully lift cookies off baking sheet and drape them over a curved form, like a wine bottle or rolling pin.

The cookie rounds will firm quickly, so if you have trouble removing them from the baking sheet, pop it in the oven for another 30 seconds, just to soften the cookies and make them workable again. Repeat the process with 4 more rounds to a batch until all the batter is used. *Makes about 2½ dozen 3-inch cookies.*

1¼ cups all-purpose flour

½ teaspoon baking soda

½ teaspoon salt

6 tablespoons unsalted butter, at room temperature

½ cup granulated sugar

1 tablespoon pure vanilla extract

1 large egg white, at room temperature

1 tablespoon vegetable or canola oil

VANILLA SNAPS

Enjoy these cookies out of hand or dunked into a glass of milk, or grind them up for the world's best vanilla cookie crust (see Vanilla Cream Pie, page 71, and Big Mama Vanilla Cheesecake, page 58).

• **Position racks in the upper and lower thirds** of the oven and preheat oven to 350°F. Line 2 baking sheets with parchment paper or silicone baking mats; have a third baking sheet ready for when it's time to freeze the cookie dough.

• **Sift together** flour, baking soda, and salt into a medium bowl. In the bowl of a stand mixer fitted with the paddle attachment, beat together butter, sugar, and vanilla extract on medium speed until light and fluffy, about 2 minutes. Add egg white and oil and continue beating until smooth, about 1 minute more. Reduce speed to low and gradually add the dry ingredients, mixing smooth.

• **Line a work surface** with a large sheet of parchment paper. Turn dough out onto parchment, pat it into a disk, and top with another sheet of parchment. With a rolling pin, roll out dough to ¼ inch thick. Leaving the dough between the sheets of parchment, transfer to the third baking sheet. Freeze until firm, about 10 minutes.

• **With a 1½-inch round cutter,** cut dough into circles, placing them 1 inch apart on the prepared baking sheets. Place sheets in the refrigerator for 10 minutes.

• **Bake until cookies** are golden on the edges, 15 to 18 minutes, rotating the sheets from front to back and top to bottom halfway through baking. Let cookies cool for 1 minute, then transfer to wire racks to cool completely.

HEIRLOOM VANILLA SUGAR COOKIES

*Makes
3 dozen
cookies*

I've been eating these cookies, an old family recipe of my gramma's, at Christmastime for my entire life. It yields the crispiest of sugar cookies: sandy textured but tender with a gorgeous pale-golden hue that begs for a smattering of colored sugar at holiday time.

- **Position racks in the upper and lower thirds** of the oven and preheat oven to 350°F. Line 2 baking sheets with parchment paper or silicone baking mats.

- **In a large bowl,** whisk together flour, baking soda, cream of tartar, and salt. In a medium bowl, whisk together oil and eggs.

- **In the bowl of a stand mixer** fitted with the paddle attachment, cream butter, granulated sugar, confectioners' sugar, and vanilla extract on medium-high speed until fluffy and pale in color, about 2 minutes. Reduce mixer speed to low and gradually beat in oil-egg mixture until smooth. Slowly add the dry ingredients and mix on low speed until smooth. The dough will be soft.

- **Roll dough into balls,** about 2 tablespoons each, and place 2 inches apart on prepared baking sheets. Pour vanilla sugar onto a plate. Dip a flat-bottom drinking glass into vanilla sugar to coat and press into each ball to flatten to about 1/4 inch thick, re-sugaring the glass each time.

- **Sprinkle flattened cookies** with decorative sugar. Bake for 10 to 12 minutes, rotating the sheets from top to bottom and front to back about halfway through, until pale golden and just beginning to turn golden brown at the edges. Let cookies cool on baking sheets for 2 minutes, then transfer to a wire rack to cool completely before storing or serving.

2 1/2 cups all-purpose flour

1/2 teaspoon baking soda

1/2 teaspoon cream of tartar

1/4 teaspoon salt

1/2 cup vegetable oil

1 large egg, at room temperature

1/2 cup (1 stick) unsalted butter, at room temperature

1/2 cup granulated sugar

1/2 cup confectioners' sugar

2 teaspoons pure vanilla extract

1/4 cup Vanilla Sugar (page 69)

Coarse rainbow sugar or other decorative sugar, for sprinkling

10 ounces white chocolate,
    chopped, divided

6   tablespoons unsalted butter,
    cut into cubes

¼   cup granulated sugar

½   teaspoon salt

2   large eggs, at room
    temperature

1   teaspoon pure
    vanilla extract

1   teaspoon vanilla
    bean paste

1   cup all-purpose flour,
    sifted

½   cup store-bought
    lemon curd*

* *You could use any well-stirred,
  low-sugar jam or preserves,
  such as orange marmalade
  or raspberry jam, instead of
  lemon curd. Any flavor that's on
  the tart side without too much
  sugar will balance the sweetness
  of the vanilla cookie base.*

LEMON-VANILLA DREAM BARS

If you love lemon bars but yearn for something a bit less messy and more portable, this recipe is a dream come true. I start with a fudgy white-chocolate base (essentially a vanilla version of the classic chocolate brownie) and swirl it with bright, tangy lemon curd. These bars are even better the day after they're baked.

• **Position a rack in the center of the oven** and preheat oven to 350°F. Coat an 8-by-8-inch pan with cooking spray and line it with a strip of parchment paper that's 8 inches wide and 14 inches long, so that there is an overhang on two sides of the pan; this will make it easier to remove the bars from the pan after baking.

• **Melt 8 ounces of the white chocolate** and butter in a heatproof bowl set over a pan of simmering water, stirring. Remove bowl from heat and stir in sugar and salt.

• **Whisk in eggs 1 at a time** and then whisk in vanilla extract and vanilla bean paste. With a spatula, gently fold in flour; when just a few streaks of flour remain, fold in the remaining 2 ounces white chocolate. Scrape batter into prepared pan.

• **Dollop lemon curd onto batter** in 5 to 6 equal portions. With a knife, swirl curd into batter with a figure-8 motion. Bake until a toothpick inserted into the center comes out clean but not dry, 25 to 28 minutes.

• **Transfer pan to a wire rack** to cool completely. Grasping the parchment overhang, lift out the entire block and cut into 12 bars.

VANILLA BISCOTTI

As a coffee lover, I'm a big fan of crunchy cookies and biscuits that can withstand a good dunking in a hot beverage. Biscotti means "twice baked"— the first bake makes the dough cakelike, and the second, at a lower temperature, crisps the cookies, giving them an addictive crunch that's perfect for a coffee break.

• **Position a rack in the center of the oven** and preheat oven to 350°F. Line a baking sheet with parchment paper or a silicone baking mat. Sift together flour, baking powder, baking soda, and salt into a large bowl.

• **In the bowl of a stand mixer** fitted with the paddle attachment, beat butter and vanilla extract on medium speed until creamy. Add sugar and beat until light in texture, about 2 minutes. Add eggs and egg white, 1 at a time, beating well after each addition. Reduce mixer speed to low and stir in flour mixture until a smooth dough forms.

• **Turn dough out** onto a lightly floured work surface and divide it in half. With floured hands, shape each half into a 7-by-2½-by-1¼-inch plank. Transfer planks to prepared sheet; they should be parallel. Bake for 30 minutes, or until dough is firm but gives when lightly pressed in the center. Let cool for 2 minutes on baking sheet and then transfer to a wire rack to cool for 15 minutes. Reduce oven temperature to 250°F.

• **Place planks on a cutting board** and, with a long serrated knife, cut on a slight diagonal into scant-½-inch slices. Return slices to the lined baking sheet. Bake until dry, firm, and crisp all over, about 1 hour. Rotate sheet 180 degrees halfway through baking and flip cookies every 15 minutes or so to encourage even drying. Transfer biscotti to a wire rack to cool.

• **To finish the cookies,** stir vanilla bean caviar into white chocolate, if using. Drizzle a bit over each cookie and refrigerate for about 10 minutes, until white chocolate is set, before serving. Store in an airtight container at room temperature for up to 3 weeks.

*Makes
2 dozen 4½-
by-1½-inch
cookies*

2½ cups all-purpose flour, plus more for shaping dough

1 teaspoon baking powder

¼ teaspoon baking soda

½ teaspoon salt

¼ cup (½ stick) unsalted butter, at room temperature

1 tablespoon plus 1 teaspoon pure vanilla extract

1 cup granulated sugar

2 large eggs plus 1 large egg white

5 ounces white chocolate, melted

Caviar of ½ vanilla bean (optional)*

* In this recipe, the vanilla caviar is mostly for appearances, though it does add a bit of flavor. Leave it out if you like, but don't substitute vanilla bean paste—it will make the melted white chocolate seize up.

VANILLA SUGAR PUFFS

Makes about 2½ dozen 2-inch puffs

These light, airy puffs, known as *chouquettes* in French, are the sort of delightful treat you can eat a dozen of in one sitting without realizing what you've done. With a few small tweaks to the recipe, you can easily make a batch of Mini Vanilla Éclairs (page 86).

• **Position racks in the upper and lower thirds** of the oven and preheat oven to 375°F. Line 2 baking sheets with parchment paper or silicone baking mats.

• **In a heavy-bottomed 2-quart saucepan,** combine milk, ½ cup water, vanilla bean, butter, sugar, and salt. Bring mixture to a simmer over medium heat, stirring occasionally. Carefully remove vanilla bean and scrape any remaining seeds into liquid. Bring mixture to a boil. Add flour, lower heat to medium, and immediately begin stirring vigorously with a wooden spoon—don't let up until the dough starts to come away from the sides of the pan and form a loose ball; a light crust will form on the bottom of the pan. Keep stirring quickly to dry the dough, about 2 minutes more. The dough should now be very smooth and have lost most of its moist appearance.

• **Transfer dough to the bowl** of a stand mixer fitted with the paddle attachment. Beat in eggs, 1 at a time, on medium speed. You'll think the dough is breaking apart and all is lost, but it will come together again when all the eggs have been added. Beat in vanilla extract. Drop dough by the tablespoonful onto prepared baking sheets, leaving about 2 inches of space between dollops.

For the dough:

- ½ cup whole milk
- 1 vanilla bean, split lengthwise
- ½ cup (1 stick) unsalted butter, cut into small pieces
- 2 tablespoons granulated sugar
- ½ teaspoon salt
- 1 cup all-purpose flour, sifted
- 5 large eggs, at room temperature
- ½ teaspoon pure vanilla extract

continued

VANILLA SUGAR PUFFS, CONT.

For decorating:

1 large egg

½ teaspoon pure
  vanilla extract

Pinch salt

Swedish pearl sugar,
to taste

- **In a small bowl,** beat together egg, vanilla extract, salt, and 1 teaspoon water until well blended. Brush each puff with this egg wash and sprinkle generously with pearl sugar.

- **Bake for 15 minutes,** then rotate the sheets from top to bottom and front to back. Continue baking until puffs are deeply golden and sound hollow when their crisp exteriors are tapped, another 15 to 20 minutes. Carefully transfer puffs to a wire rack to cool a bit before serving.

Viva Vanilla!

Mini Vanilla Éclairs: In spite of their sexy slick of chocolate ganache, éclairs have always seemed like a vanilla recipe to me, with the chocolate playing second fiddle to all that creamy vanilla filling. After beating in the eggs and vanilla extract, transfer the dough to a piping bag and pipe it into 2½-inch lengths. Bake as above and, when cool, fill with a batch of Modern Vanilla Pastry Cream (page 125). Load the pastry cream into a pastry bag fitted with a medium round tip. Pierce one side of each éclair with the tip and fill it slowly, just until you feel the weight of the filling inside the éclair. For the ganache, combine 4 ounces chopped bittersweet chocolate and ½ cup heavy cream in a heatproof bowl. Melt together in the microwave with 30-second bursts of high power, stirring well after each interval, just until the glaze is smooth. Spoon ganache onto the filled éclairs and refrigerate until ganache is set before serving.

HOMEMADE VANILLA EXTRACT

Homemade vanilla extract is one of those glorious things that cause people to marvel at your Martha-esque domestic skills. It's both terrific party-conversation fodder and an economical way to enjoy copious amounts of pure vanilla extract.

And it couldn't be simpler. All you need is a clean jar or bottle with a tight-fitting lid, whole vanilla beans, and a clear neutral-tasting liquor (vodka is my top choice). For an 8-ounce jar, 2 split beans should do, but you can add more if you like. Let the sealed jar sit in a cool, dark place for about 2 months before using. I also add scraped seedpods to the extract jar after I've used them in recipes, unless they land in my container of Vanilla Sugar first (page 69). As you use the extract, top off the jar with more of the same type of liquor for a nearly never-ending supply.

Aside from being a great way to save money on a pricey ingredient, making your own extract is a an excellent opportunity to use some of the more exotic flavors of whole beans in liquid form, since store-bought extracts rarely come in such varieties. Magical! You can also combine several different varieties of vanilla in one batch of extract, creating your own special blends. Few things make a more fabulous edible gift than homemade vanilla extract in a vintage bottle decorated with a darling handmade tag. Martha's got nuthin' on you.

SALTED VANILLA CHIP OATMEAL COOKIES

*Makes
3 dozen 3-inch
cookies*

I'm not trying to start an all-out war, so I won't dare suggest that a vanilla-chip cookie could dethrone the classic chocolate-chip variety forever. But, between you and me, this earthy, sweet-salty, nubbly little number is every bit as addictive as its perennially popular cousin.

- **Position racks in the upper and lower thirds** of the oven and preheat oven to 350°F. Line 2 baking sheets with parchment paper or silicone baking mats.

- **In a large bowl,** whisk oats, flour, baking soda, and salt to blend well.

- **In the bowl of a stand mixer** fitted with the paddle attachment, beat butter and vanilla extract on medium-high speed until blended and creamy. Add sugars and beat until light and fluffy, about 2 minutes.

- **Beat in eggs 1 at a time.** Reduce mixer speed to low and gradually add oat mixture, then white chocolate.

- **Scoop batter,** 2 tablespoons at a time, onto prepared baking sheets, about 8 cookies to a sheet. Sprinkle a bit of vanilla fleur de sel onto each cookie.

- **Bake until cookies are golden** around the edges but still a bit soft in the centers, 12 to 14 minutes, rotating sheets from front to back and top to bottom halfway through baking. Do not overbake. Let cookies cool on sheets for 2 minutes and them transfer to a wire rack to cool completely.

3 cups old-fashioned rolled oats

1½ cups all-purpose flour

1 teaspoon baking soda

¾ teaspoon salt

¾ cup (1½ sticks) unsalted butter, at room temperature

1 tablespoon pure vanilla extract

⅔ cup dark brown sugar, packed

⅔ cup granulated sugar

2 large eggs, at room temperature

8 ounces white chocolate, chopped*

2 tablespoons Vanilla Fleur de Sel (page 90), for sprinkling

You can use white chocolate chips, but the flavor and texture of chopped chunks from a good-quality bar of white chocolate can't be beat.

VANILLA FLEUR DE SEL

Sweet foods are perfect with a kick of vanilla, and I've already waxed poetic about the glorious muse that is Homemade Vanilla Sugar (page 69). But what about giving salt a hint of vanilla, too? There's no reason this dreamy, rich flavor—especially in bolder varieties from Tonga and India—can't go savory. Vanilla Fleur de Sel is delicious as a finishing salt sprinkled over many savory dishes (like fish and delicate seafoods, spring vegetables, and green salads that incorporate seasonal fruit or berries). It's also an exquisite final touch on cookies, brownies, and caramels (see Salted Vanilla Chip Oatmeal Cookies, page 89, and Vanilla Bean-Sea Salt Caramels, page 105, for some sweet and salty inspiration).

All you need is a box of good flaky sea salt (I love Maldon Sea Salt Flakes) and a whole, split vanilla bean or two. Put them in a lidded jar and shake it every couple of days, letting the vanilla penetrate and perfume the salt for a week or so. The result is a parcel of unexpected culinary genius that makes the perfect gift for those perennially unimpressed foodies in your life.

❋ As a general rule, use about 1 cup of flaky sea salt per bean.

VANILLA BEAN MERINGUE KISSES

Makes 4 dozen 1½-inch kisses

Meringue nears the top of my list of Best Foods on the Entire Planet. It's so beautiful and delicious in its simplicity and serves as a backdrop for so many different flavors and add-ins. But, as a purist, I find its angelic texture and melting sweetness ideal for showcasing—what else?— pure vanilla flavor.

- **Position oven racks in the upper and lower thirds** of the oven and preheat oven to 200°F. Line 2 baking sheets with parchment paper.

- **In the bowl of a stand mixer** fitted with the whisk attachment, beat together egg whites, cream of tartar, and salt on medium-high speed until very foamy and just barely holding shape, about 2 minutes.

- **Sift sugars together into a small bowl** and then gradually add sugars to egg-white mixture, continuing to beat until batter holds firm peaks, about 3 minutes more. Increase mixer speed to high and beat for 1 final minute, adding vanilla extract and vanilla bean caviar.

- **Transfer meringue** to a pastry bag fitted with a large round or star tip.

- **Pipe meringues** about 1½ inches in diameter on prepared baking sheets, leaving about 1 inch between them. Bake until meringues are firm and crisp, about 1½ hours. Turn off oven,

continued

4 large egg whites, at room temperature

¼ teaspoon cream of tartar

¼ teaspoon salt

½ cup granulated sugar

½ cup confectioners' sugar

1½ teaspoons pure vanilla extract

Caviar of ½ vanilla bean

VANILLA BEAN MERINGUE KISSES, CONT.

open the door slightly, and let meringues cool completely in oven, about 1 hour more. Store in an airtight container for up to 1 week.

Use this same recipe as the base for Vanilla Mascarpone Pavlova (page 72).

Viva Vanilla!

Vanilla-Almond Meringue Bark: Instead of piping the meringue, spread it in an even layer about ⅓ inch thick on a large, parchment-paper-lined baking sheet. Sprinkle sliced almonds over it and bake until the meringue is dry and crisp, about 1 hour. Let cool completely in the oven, with the door open a bit, before breaking into pieces.

VANILLA CRÈME COOKIE SANDWICHES

Makes 2 dozen filled sandwich cookies

Sandwich cookies are a delicious, totally acceptable way to eat two cookies at once. This recipe features two vanilla shortbreads fused together with a dollop of vanilla bean–white chocolate ganache.

• **Begin by making the filling.** In a medium heatproof bowl, combine white chocolate and cream. Microwave in 30-second bursts on medium power, stirring well after each interval, until white chocolate is melted and mixture is smooth. Stir in vanilla caviar. Let cool and thicken at room temperature for 2 to 3 hours. (Short on time? Refrigerate mixture for about 30 minutes, stirring often, until cooled and thickened).

• **To make the cookies,** sift together flour, salt, and baking soda into a large bowl.

• **In the bowl of a stand mixer** fitted with the paddle attachment, beat butter, sugar, and vanilla extract together on medium speed until light and fluffy, about 2 minutes. Beat in egg until well blended, then add egg yolk. Reduce mixer speed to low and stir in flour mixture.

• **Turn dough out** onto a lightly floured work surface and divide it in half. Shape each half into a log about 8 inches long and 1½ inches in diameter. Wrap each log in plastic wrap and refrigerate until firm, at least 2 to 3 hours. (At this point the dough can be frozen and stored for up to 6 months.)

For the filling:

8 ounces white chocolate, chopped

⅓ cup heavy cream

Caviar of ½ vanilla bean*

For the cookies:

2 cups all-purpose flour

½ teaspoon salt

¼ teaspoon baking soda

¾ cup (1½ sticks) unsalted butter, at room temperature

½ cup granulated sugar

1 tablespoon pure vanilla extract

1 large egg plus 1 large egg yolk

*Make sure to use vanilla caviar instead of vanilla bean paste, which—like the addition of a drop of any liquid—might make the ganache seize into one big grainy mass, rendering it unusable.

continued

VANILLA CRÈME COOKIE SANDWICHES, CONT.

• **Position racks in the upper and lower thirds** of the oven and preheat oven to 350°F. Line 2 baking sheets with parchment paper or silicone baking mats.

• **Slice dough into rounds** slightly less than ¼ inch thick and place rounds about 1 inch apart on prepared baking sheets. Bake until cookies are firm at the edges and just beginning to turn lightly golden, 17 to 20 minutes. Let cool on baking sheets for 2 minutes and then transfer to wire racks to cool completely.

• **For each cookie sandwich,** spread about 2 teaspoons of filling on the bottom of a cookie, top with a second cookie, and press gently to adhere.

Viva Vanilla!

Tuxedo Crème Cookie Sandwiches: For a double-stuffed treat, combine 8 ounces bittersweet chocolate and ½ cup heavy cream in a heatproof bowl. Melt together in the microwave with 30-second bursts of high power, stirring well after each interval, just until the mixture is smooth. Let thicken at room temperature for about 30 minutes. Pipe a thin layer of chocolate ganache on top of the vanilla crème before closing sandwich.

CANDIES & CONFECTIONS

When I was a kid, I treated candy bars like a science-class dissection—with gapped teeth I'd gnaw off the chocolate coating, then the nuts, and finally the caramel, determined to be left with an unadorned slab of irresistible vanilla nougat (my favorite part) to savor on its own. Now that I am a grown-up and simply can't be bothered with such inefficiency, I've developed a recipe for Vanilla Nougat Candy Bar Bites: a hunk of nougat with a bit of chocolate and nuts to balance everything out. A reverse-engineered candy bar, if you will. That recipe has given way to many other candies and confections that bring vanilla to the forefront.

VANILLA BEAN MARSHMALLOWS

Makes 4 dozen 1½-inch marshmallows

My first cookbook was all about homemade marshmallows, and while writing it I lived and breathed (and scrubbed my kitchen floor clean of) that sweet, bouncy confection for months on end. Even after testing dozens of exotic and delicious flavors, I still consider the classic vanilla marshmallow to be the ultimate.

- **Coat a 9-by-13-inch baking pan** lightly with cooking spray and wipe away any excess.

- **Whisk together** gelatin and 1 cup of the cold water in a small bowl and let stand for at least 5 minutes, until gelatin softens.

- **Stir together** sugar, ½ cup of the corn syrup, the remaining ½ cup cold water, and salt in a medium saucepan over high heat. Boil, stirring occasionally, until the temperature reaches 240°F.

- **Meanwhile, pour the remaining** ½ cup corn syrup into the bowl of a stand mixer fitted with the whisk attachment. Microwave gelatin mixture on high power until it is completely melted, about 30 seconds. Pour it into mixer bowl and set mixer to low speed.

- **Once syrup mixture reaches 240°F,** remove it from heat. Slowly pour into mixer bowl in a steady stream, aiming for the space between the beater and the bowl. Increase mixer speed to medium and beat for 5 minutes. Increase speed to medium-

3 tablespoons unflavored powdered gelatin

1½ cups cold water, divided

1½ cups granulated sugar

1 cup light corn syrup, divided

¼ teaspoon salt

1 tablespoon pure vanilla extract

1 teaspoon vanilla bean paste

½ cup confectioners' sugar

½ cup cornstarch

continued

high and beat for 5 more minutes. Turn mixer to the highest setting and beat for 1 to 2 minutes more; beat in vanilla extract and vanilla bean paste. At this point, the marshmallow will be opaque white, fluffy, and roughly tripled in volume.

• **Pour marshmallow into prepared pan.** Use an offset spatula to nudge it into the corners and smooth the top.

• **Sift confectioners' sugar and cornstarch** together into a medium bowl. Sift mixture evenly and generously over the top of the marshmallow; reserve leftover coating (you will need it when cutting marshmallow after it sets). Let set for at least 6 hours in a cool, dry place.

• **Run a knife around the edges** of the pan to loosen marshmallow. Invert the entire slab onto a coating-dusted work surface and dust marshmallow with more coating. Cut into whatever size pieces you wish (a pizza cutter works great for making squares). Dip the sticky edges of the marshmallows in more coating, patting off excess.

Viva Vanilla!

Vanilla-Berry Marshmallows: Omit the 1 cup cold water in the first step and soften the gelatin in 1 cup cold, strained raspberry, strawberry, or blackberry puree.

Chocolate-Dipped Marshmallows: Melt 8 ounces bittersweet chocolate in a double boiler or the microwave. Dip each cut marshmallow halfway into chocolate, tapping off excess. Set on a parchment-paper-lined baking sheet and let chocolate set before serving.

VANILLA BUTTER MINTS

Makes about 10 dozen ½-inch candies

These mints are reminiscent of the kind found at diners and baby showers, but they have a much softer, melting texture and more vanilla flavor, with just a hint of mint. Color them to fit a party theme or roll out the dough and cut into shapes with small fondant cutters instead of the classic butter mint shape.

- **Sift together** ¼ cup of the confectioners' sugar and 4 tablespoons of the cornstarch into a medium bowl.

- **In the bowl of a stand mixer** fitted with the paddle attachment, beat the remaining 2½ cups confectioners' sugar, the remaining 2 tablespoons cornstarch, butter, milk, extracts, and salt on medium speed until a smooth dough forms, about 1½ minutes. If you wish to color the mints, add a few drops of food coloring.

- **Generously dust a work surface** and a large baking sheet with the reserved sugar-cornstarch mixture. Turn the candy dough out onto work surface and divide into 4 pieces. Roll each piece into a long rope about ½ inch in diameter. Slice into ½-inch lengths and transfer to prepared baking sheet.

- **Refrigerate candies** until dry and firm, about 4 hours. Store in an airtight container in single layers between sheets of parchment or waxed paper.

2¾ cups confectioners' sugar, sifted, divided

6 tablespoons cornstarch, divided

¼ cup (½ stick) unsalted butter, at room temperature

1 tablespoon milk

2 teaspoons pure vanilla extract

¼ teaspoon pure peppermint extract

¼ teaspoon salt

Food coloring, optional

VANILLA NOUGAT CANDY BAR BITES

*Makes about
2 dozen
1-inch bites*

See the introduction to this chapter (page 97) for the inspiration behind these sweet little morsels.

• **Lightly coat a 9-by-5-inch loaf pan** with cooking spray. Line it with parchment paper and lightly spray the parchment, too.

• **In a medium heavy-bottomed saucepan** over medium-high heat, stir together sugar, ½ cup water, corn syrup, and salt. Boil until the temperature reaches 238°F.

• **Meanwhile, in the bowl of a stand mixer** fitted with the whisk attachment, whip egg whites on medium speed until they hold soft peaks, about 2 minutes. With the mixer on medium speed, slowly pour half of the hot syrup into egg whites, beginning with just 1 to 2 tablespoons and then gradually pouring in the rest (adding just a little syrup at first warms up the egg whites and prevents them from scrambling). Immediately return saucepan with the remaining hot syrup to medium-high heat and bring to a boil; continue beating egg-white mixture until thick, with the consistency of marshmallow crème, then beat in vanilla bean paste and vanilla extract and turn off mixer.

• **When the syrup temperature reaches 275°F,** turn mixer on at medium speed and slowly pour in syrup. Increase mixer speed to high and beat for 10 to 12 minutes, until mixture is very thick, heavy, and beginning to lose its gloss; the bowl should be cool except for the very bottom. Scrape mixture into prepared pan and spread it into the corners with lightly oiled hands or an offset spatula. Let set at room temperature until completely cool and firm, about 2 hours.

continued

1⅔ cups granulated sugar

⅓ cup light corn syrup

½ teaspoon salt

2 large egg whites, at room temperature

2 teaspoons vanilla bean paste

1 teaspoon pure vanilla extract

2 ounces bittersweet chocolate (60 to 70 percent cacao), melted

¼ cup finely chopped salted nuts*

* *Use whatever kind of nuts you like. Salted peanuts and almonds are especially good for a candy-bar effect.*

VANILLA NOUGAT CANDY BAR BITES, CONT.

• **Invert nougat onto a cutting surface** and remove the parchment. The slab should be sticky side up (the side that was exposed to the air while setting should be dry and not sticky when touched). Cut into 1-inch squares and place squares sticky side up on a parchment-paper-lined baking sheet. Pour melted chocolate into a small zip-top bag. Use scissors to snip off the corner of the bag. Drizzle a bit of chocolate over each nougat square and sprinkle chopped nuts on top. Refrigerate until chocolate is set, about 5 minutes, before serving.

If the egg whites hold soft peaks before the syrup temperature reaches 238°F, stop the mixer—you want the whipped whites to be ready and waiting for the syrup, not the other way around.

This soft nougat is the perfect base for all kinds of creative confection. Flavor it as you like (peppermint holiday nougat, anyone?), fold in dried fruits and nuts for a riff on Italian torrone, or use it as inspiration for your own homemade candy bars.

VANILLA BEAN-SEA SALT CARAMELS

*4 dozen
1-by-1½-inch
candies*

I am caramel obsessed. **Chewy, saucy, crunchy, whatever—I love it all, and I make it often. Any good caramel recipe includes a splash of vanilla to heighten the flavor of the caramelized sugar. But in this recipe, the vanilla flavor is the star. The secret is to steep the bean in the cream, which permeates the entire pot of caramel with pure vanilla flavor.**

½ cup heavy cream

½ vanilla bean, split lengthwise*

6 tablespoons unsalted butter, cut into pieces

1 cup granulated sugar

¼ cup light brown sugar, packed

½ cup light corn syrup

2 teaspoons coarse, flaky sea salt, plus more for sprinkling**

1 teaspoon vanilla bean paste

* *An extra-bold variety of vanilla, such as Indian, will cut through the richness of these creamy caramels.*

** *I'm a huge fan Maldon sea salt flakes; Vanilla Fleur de Sel (page 90) is also delicious in this recipe.*

• **Line an 8-by-8-inch baking pan** with aluminum foil and coat it with nonstick cooking spray.

• **In a medium heavy-bottom saucepan** over medium-high heat, combine the cream and vanilla bean. Heat until mixture just begins to simmer around the edges—do not boil. Remove from heat, cover pan, and let steep for 15 minutes.

• **Remove vanilla bean** and scrape the caviar into the cream, discarding the pod. Add butter, sugars, corn syrup, and salt. Bring mixture to a boil over medium-high heat, stirring until the sugar dissolves. Clip a candy thermometer to the pot and reduce heat to low, stirring occasionally, until temperature reaches 242°F. Remove pan from heat and stir in vanilla bean paste.

• **Pour mixture** into the prepared pan set over a wire rack. Let caramel cool undisturbed at room temperature overnight (or 30 minutes at room temperature and another 30 minutes or so in the refrigerator) until very firm.

continued

VANILLA BEAN-SEA SALT CARAMELS, CONT.

• **Line a cutting surface** with a sheet of parchment paper and turn the caramel slab out onto it.

• **Use a large, sharp knife** to cut neat, even pieces, each about 1 by 1½ inches. Garnish with a sprinkling of salt, if you like. Wrap caramels in squares of parchment or waxed paper. Store at room temperature.

Cupcake papers are a timesaving alternative to cutting squares of parchment for wrapping the caramels.

When making candy, vanilla bean paste is a go-to ingredient. Though I usually recommend using whole beans when working with hot liquids (in which the beans can be steeped), the sugar syrups involved in candy-making get way too hot, and fishing out the bean pods can be dangerous business. Vanilla bean paste is an excellent alternative here: it gives both the great flavor you'd get from an extract and pretty vanilla bean flecks for aesthetics.

Viva Vanilla!

Sea Salt Caramels in the Raw: For a wonderfully complex and unrefined take on this confection, swap out the white and brown sugars for 1¼ cups turbinado sugar. Instead of the corn syrup, use ⅓ cup light agave nectar. Cook the caramel until it reaches 248°F before proceeding with the rest of the recipe as usual.

CANDIED VANILLA POPCORN

Makes about
4 quarts

This sweet and salty treat tends to disappear moments after I set it out for my guests. I also like to add a few drops of food coloring to the sugar syrup and then pile the popcorn in tall glass jars for a sort of edible party decoration.

12 cups popped popcorn (from about ½ cup unpopped kernels)*

Salt, to taste, plus ⅛ teaspoon salt, for the syrup

1 cup roasted salted peanuts

1½ cups granulated sugar

½ cup light corn syrup

2 teaspoons vanilla bean paste

¼ teaspoon almond extract

4 ounces white chocolate, melted

I like oil-popping my popcorn the old-fashioned way in a big, heavy-bottomed pot on the stovetop. But air-popped or even good-quality microwave popcorn works fine.

• **Preheat oven to 300°F.** Line a large rimmed baking sheet with a silicone baking mat, or line with foil and coat foil with nonstick cooking spray.

• **Season popcorn with salt to taste** and discard any unpopped kernels. Combine popcorn with peanuts on prepared baking sheet and keep it warm in oven while you prepare the syrup.

• **In a medium, heavy-bottomed saucepan,** combine sugar, corn syrup, and ½ cup water and stir gently. Bring mixture to a boil over medium-high heat. Clip a candy thermometer to the side of the pan and boil mixture, stirring occasionally, until the temperature reaches 300°F.

• **Remove pan from heat;** set thermometer aside. Stir in vanilla bean paste, almond extract, and the ⅛ teaspoon salt. Remove baking sheet from oven and quickly pour the syrup over popcorn and peanuts in a thin, steady stream. Wearing heatproof gloves or using two wooden spoons, immediately toss popcorn to coat. Pat everything into an even layer and drizzle white chocolate over top. Let cool completely on baking sheet. When white chocolate has set, break into pieces. Store in an airtight container for up to 1 week.

Frosted Vanilla Almonds, Opera Fudge,
and Vanilla Bean-Sea Salt Caramels,
recipes pages 111, 109, and 105

OPERA FUDGE

Makes
about 2½ dozen
½-ounce
candies

If you hail from anywhere near Lebanon, Pennsylvania, you will most likely recognize this dainty confection, which is native to that area. Although it's a bit of an undertaking, even with the streamlining I've done in this recipe, it's so fun to make and perfect for holiday candy-making. Opera Fudge's creamy, light texture is really more like that of a fondant or vanilla buttercream candy filling than a true fudge, but that's neither here nor there, because this stuff is so, so good.

2 cups granulated sugar

¾ cup heavy cream

¼ cup whole milk

1 tablespoon light corn syrup

½ teaspoon salt

2 tablespoons unsalted butter, cut into thin slices

2 teaspoons vanilla bean paste

3 ounces unsweetened chocolate, chopped

4 ounces bittersweet chocolate (60 to 70 percent cacao), chopped, divided

• **In a medium, heavy-bottomed saucepan,** stir together sugar, cream, milk, corn syrup, and salt. Gently stir mixture over medium heath just until it comes to a boil. Stop stirring and clip a candy thermometer onto the side of the pan. When the temperature reaches 220°F, drop the pieces of butter evenly over the surface, but do not stir. Raise heat to high just until mixture boils again and then reduce it to medium. Continue boiling until temperature reaches 238°F.

• **Remove pan from heat** but leave thermometer in the candy mixture. Let cool to about 170°F.

• **Line a baking sheet with a silicone baking mat** or parchment paper lightly coated with nonstick cooking spray. Slowly pour candy mixture into the bowl of a stand mixer fitted with the paddle attachment; do not scrape the pan. Add vanilla bean paste.

When pouring the candy from the saucepan into the mixing bowl, you can gently coax the mixture out of the pan with a flexible spatula, but be careful not to scrape the sides or bottom of the pan. Fudge loves to find wayward sugar crystals

continued

OPERA FUDGE, CONT.

and then promptly seize up into an inedible ball. That's also why you should not stir the candy once it has come to a boil.

• **Turn mixer to lowest setting and mix** for about 7 to 8 minutes. During this time, the fudge will cool, thicken, become lighter in color, and begin to take on a claylike texture. After 7 minutes, turn off the mixer and scoop out a little bit of the candy. When it holds its shape but both the mixture and the bowl are still warm, it's ready to form into balls. If it doesn't hold its shape, continue to mix for 30 seconds at a time and then try scooping it again.

• **Using a small 1-teaspoon scoop** or two spoons, scoop candy into small balls, rolling each one with your palms. Place balls on prepared baking sheet and let fudge stand at room temperature until cool and firm, at least 2 hours.

• **In a double boiler or the microwave,** melt unsweetened chocolate and 2 ounces of the bittersweet chocolate, stirring occasionally. Add the remaining 2 ounces bittersweet chocolate and continue stirring until melted. Dip each fudge ball in chocolate, tapping off excess, and return to baking sheet. Let chocolate set before serving.

As it cools, the fudge will go from a malleable claylike substance to something sort of crumbly and difficult, so you'll want to try to work quickly when rolling it into balls. Making sure the bowl is still warm when you turn off the mixer will buy you some time.

The blend of unsweetened and bittersweet chocolates in the coating gives these candies an elegant edge, but don't be fooled—the creamy vanilla confection in the center is the real star.

FROSTED VANILLA ALMONDS

*Makes about
3½ cups*

These toasty, sugary, dangerously addictive almonds are reminiscent of the ones served warm in paper cones at carnivals and fairs. In a beribboned Mason jar or cellophane bag, they make a scrumptious edible gift.

2 large egg whites,
  at room temperature

⅔ cup granulated sugar

1 tablespoon plus 1 teaspoon
  pure vanilla extract

½ teaspoon salt

3 cups raw almonds*

* *Be sure to use raw almonds.
  Nuts that are already roasted
  will burn during baking.*

• **Position a rack in the center of the oven** and preheat oven to 300°F. Line a large rimmed baking sheet with parchment paper or a silicone baking mat.

• **In a large bowl,** whisk together egg whites, sugar, vanilla extract, and salt until well blended and foamy. Fold in almonds until coated. Pour onto prepared baking sheet and smooth into an even layer.

• **Bake for 10 minutes,** then stir well (being sure to pat the almonds into an even layer), rotate baking sheet 180 degrees, and bake until crisp and just beginning to turn golden, about 20 minutes more.

• **Transfer the almonds** with the parchment or silicone mat to a wire rack to cool a bit. Serve warm, or let cool completely and store in an airtight container.

GOLDEN PEAR-VANILLA JAM

*Makes 6
half-pint jars*

Vanilla lovers, this jam's for you. Cooked pears are wonderfully neutral and let the vanilla shine.

6 cups peeled, cored, and chopped pears (from about 5 medium pears)

4 cups granulated sugar, divided

2 tablespoons freshly squeezed lemon juice

2 vanilla beans, split lengthwise

1 1.75-ounce package powdered pectin

• **In a canning pot** or other large pot big enough to hold 6 half-pint jars, boil the jars in water for 10 minutes to sterilize. Remove from heat, drop in the jar lids, and cover pot to keep jars and lids hot while you make the jam.

• **In a large, heavy-bottomed pot,** such as a Dutch oven, combine pears, 3¾ cups of the sugar, lemon juice, and vanilla beans. Bring to a boil over medium heat, stirring often. Boil until pears are very tender, 12 to 15 minutes, mashing with a potato masher as the fruit softens.

• **In a small bowl,** whisk together the remaining ¼ cup sugar and pectin and then stir into pear mixture. Boil for 5 minutes more, stirring occasionally. Remove vanilla bean pods and scrape any remaining caviar into the jam.

• **Using canning tongs,** carefully remove jars and lids from hot water and transfer to a work surface covered with a clean dish towel; place pot with the water over medium heat. Dry jars and lids and then immediately ladle jam into jars. Wipe the rims clean with a clean, damp cloth. Close jars tightly. When water reaches a rolling boil, add filled, closed jars to the pot, adding more water if necessary to cover jars by a few inches. Boil for 10 minutes. Return jars to dish towel to cool, and check that they have sealed properly before storing (the center of each lids should not make a popping sound when pressed with a fingertip). The jam can be stored for 1 year; once opened, it keeps for about 1 month in the refrigerator.

It's rare that a random jar won't seal, but if it happens you can refrigerate it or transfer the contents to a clean, sterilized jar, recap it, and process it again.

VANILLA LOLLIPOPS

The flavor of these pops is a cross between cotton candy and light caramel, with lots of vanilla mixed in. In other words, totally crave-worthy.

- **Line 2 baking sheets** with silicone baking mats. Set 5 to 6 lollipop sticks on each sheet, leaving plenty of space between them. Coat a large, heatproof spouted measuring cup with nonstick cooking spray.

- **In a small bowl,** whisk together cream and vanilla bean paste. In a medium saucepan, stir together sugar, ½ cup water, corn syrup, salt, and cream of tartar. Bring mixture to a boil over medium-high heat. Clip a candy thermometer onto the side of the pan. Boil mixture until the temperature reaches about 295°F; immediately remove from heat and let temperature continue to rise to 300°F (this will happen fairly quickly). Carefully add cream mixture and whisk vigorously until smooth. Scrape syrup into prepared measuring cup.

- **Working quickly and carefully,** pour a round puddle of syrup, about 3 inches in diameter, over the top third of each lollipop stick. Pour syrup in a steady stream, moving the cup around in a circular motion as necessary to form as neat a circle as possible (it will probably take you a couple of pops to get the hang of it).

- **Let candy set** for about 1 hour before eating or wrapping lollipops.

Package these lollipops sweetly in a small cellophane bag tied with a ribbon bow.

Makes 10 to 12
3-inch pops

2	tablespoons heavy cream
2	teaspoons vanilla bean paste
1	cup granulated sugar
⅓	cup corn syrup
⅛	teaspoon salt
⅛	teaspoon cream of tartar
10 to 12 lollipop sticks	

THROW A VANILLA TASTING PARTY

As with different varieties of wine, the flavors and characteristics of vanilla are influenced by the part of the world and the conditions in which the species is grown. Experience them all by trying different varieties of vanilla and places of origin (see page 19). Creating a spread of multiple types to sample is a fun and eye-opening way to taste and compare many different flavors at once (like a wine-tasting party—minus the hangover).

I don't recommend eating scraped vanilla caviar straight from the bean or gnawing on a bean pod—because of its intensity, vanilla in this form is less than appetizing. And slurping a spoonful of extract will leave you with a burning alcohol sensation, not delicious vanilla flavor. Instead, use a vehicle for the vanilla, such as your favorite neutral-tasting butter or shortbread cookie recipe (like the Heirloom Vanilla Sugar Cookies on page 81); make a few small batches of dough and use a different variety of vanilla in each. That way, each vanilla can bloom and reveal the beautiful, delicious little facets that make it unique.

To really home in on the vanilla itself, milk is absolutely the perfect backdrop—its neutral flavor has just a hint of sweetness. Cold milk is best because it's more neutral in flavor; warm milk tastes milkier. And because fat can coat the tongue and dull the taste buds as you move through the tasting, skim milk is ideal.

If you have different extracts on hand, simply stir one into cold milk, about ¾ to 1 teaspoon extract per 8 ounces milk. If you're working with whole beans (many of the world's most exotic and interesting-tasting vanillas come only in this form), you'll have to warm the milk and steep the pods to really bring out the vanilla essence: For each whole bean, pour 2 cups skim milk into a small saucepan. Split bean lengthwise and add to milk. Over medium heat, scald milk (steam will begin to rise from the pot and tiny bubbles will start to form around the edge; don't let milk simmer). Remove from heat, cover pot, and let steep for 10 minutes. Pour milk and pod into a labeled heatproof container, cover, and refrigerate until cold before tasting. Wash out the pot before making another batch with a different vanilla variety to keep the flavor pure.

When it's time to taste, have plenty of fresh water on hand for cleansing palates between tastings. Pour small amounts of each vanilla-flavored milk into small glasses (shot glasses are ideal). Label the glasses or do a blind tasting. Instruct tasters to sip and swish the milk around their mouths before swallowing. To get really serious, give guests small notepads available to write down their thoughts as they taste. You just might foster a group of future vanilla snobs.

CUSTARDS & CREAMS

I think when most of us dream about the perfect vanilla treat, we envision something sweet and creamy, cozy and comforting, with the sort of texture that reflects the flavor of vanilla itself. Ice creams, puddings, a silky sea of vanilla custard under the crackling burnt sugar crust of a crème brûlée—this chapter's recipes are the stuff of vanilla dreams. Even better, most allow you to use the entire vanilla bean and eke out every last bit of flavor.

TANGY VANILLA BEAN PANNA COTTA

Serves
6

The beauty of panna cotta, aside from its simplicity and incredible ease of preparation, is how easily you can adjust the richness and sweetness to suit your taste. The following proportions of heavy cream, buttermilk, and sour cream yield just the right level of richness for me, but you can adjust the amounts of these ingredients according to your preference. I love using Tahitian vanilla beans in this recipe and serving the finished panna cottas with a variety of seasonal fruits.

2 tablespoons cold water

2 teaspoons unflavored powdered gelatin

2 cups heavy cream

⅓ cup granulated sugar

1 vanilla bean, split lengthwise

¼ teaspoon salt

1 cup well-shaken buttermilk*

1 cup sour cream

* *Buttermilk provides a lighter, but still luxuriously textured, alternative to cream and, when combined with the sour cream, gives a refreshing tang to what is often a heavy dessert. I also think the slightly sour notes make the vanilla flavor shine.*

• **In a small bowl,** whisk together cold water and gelatin and let soften for 5 minutes.

• **In a medium saucepan,** combine heavy cream, sugar, vanilla bean, and salt. Cook over medium-low heat, stirring often to dissolve sugar, until mixture is hot (don't let it boil!). Remove from heat and whisk in gelatin mixture until smooth. Let mixture cool for 5 to 10 minutes. Remove vanilla bean and scrape the caviar into pan, discarding the pod.

• **In a large bowl,** whisk together buttermilk and sour cream and then whisk into heavy cream mixture until smooth. Divide mixture equally among 6 6-ounce ramekins, custard cups, or coffee cups. Chill, uncovered, until firm, 3 to 4 hours. To serve, unmold panna cottas onto dessert dishes or serve straight from the ramekins in which they were chilled.

Viva Vanilla!

Honey-Vanilla Panna Cotta: Reduce granulated sugar to ¼ cup and add ¼ cup honey along with the sugar.

6 cups whole milk

⅔ cup medium-grain white rice*

⅓ cup granulated sugar

1 vanilla bean, split lengthwise
and caviar scraped

¾ teaspoon salt

* *Note that this recipe calls for medium-grain white rice (not long- or short-grain rice), which lends the perfect amount of starch, creaminess, and texture to the finished pudding.*

CREAMY VANILLA RICE PUDDING

Nothing is quite as cozy and homey as a bowl of creamy vanilla pudding. Simple dishes like this are also the perfect way to showcase a flavorful, high-quality vanilla. This pudding can be served chilled or slightly warm—it will appear quite soupy at the end of cooking but will thicken considerably during its time in the fridge.

• **In a large, heavy-bottomed pot,** combine milk, rice, sugar, vanilla caviar and pod, and salt. Bring to a simmer over medium heat, stirring gently. Cover pot, reduce heat to low, and simmer for 15 minutes. Uncover pot and continue to cook, stirring often, until rice is very tender and pudding has thickened slightly, about 15 minutes more. Remove pot from heat and let pudding cool for 5 minutes before transferring to a heatproof bowl. Refrigerate until cold and thick, at least 4 hours or as long as overnight.

Viva Vanilla!

Warm Vanilla-Rum Rice Pudding: Give this pudding a warm, boozy glow by whisking in two large egg yolks and adding a shot of dark rum during the last 5 minutes of cooking.

HOMEMADE VANILLA COFFEE CREAMER

You know what drives my husband nuts? What he calls "lady coffee"—any coffee that has a creamy look and is flavored. He can smell when such a coffee beverage has been created in our kitchen before he even enters the house. Unfortunately for him, I happen to love lady coffee. For a while, the only thing that kept me from always making lady coffee (besides the Man whining about it) was the high price and somewhat questionable ingredients in the flavored coffee creamers from the supermarket. Then I figured out that I could make my own for a fraction of the cost and with much simpler, and more natural, ingredients. Sorry, honey.

    1 14-ounce can sweetened condensed milk
1½ cups milk, half-and-half, or heavy cream
    1 whole vanilla bean, split lengthwise
      Pinch of salt

In a small saucepan, combine all ingredients. Warm over medium heat until mixture is hot and steaming, but not simmering. Remove from heat, cover, and let steep for 15 minutes. Strain into a jar or other container with a tight-fitting lid. Store in the refrigerator for up to 2 weeks. *Makes about 2 cups*

❋ Vanilla coffee creamer is delicious, but you can also use cinnamon, ginger, nutmeg, or any combination of spices. Add them when the milk is hot and give them time to steep along with the vanilla bean. Extracts like peppermint or almond, added to taste right before straining, are fabulous. And of course a few tablespoons of high-quality cocoa powder makes a divine mocha creamer. Pour into cute jars for a fun hostess gift!

MODERN VANILLA PASTRY CREAM

Makes about
3 cups

Vanilla pastry cream is the backbone of so many desserts, such as filled cakes, tarts, cream puffs (profiteroles), and Napoleons (mille-feuille). It's a staple in professional pastry kitchens, but because it's so versatile, you'll want to keep this recipe in your back pocket. I've updated the classic by increasing the vanilla flavor (of course), reducing the sugar, and lightening things up by replacing some of the egg yolks with a whole egg. Traditionally, the cooked custard is strained through a sieve, but I find that a blender makes the cream perfectly light and smooth.

2 cups whole milk

½ vanilla bean, split lengthwise

1 large egg plus 4 large egg yolks

½ cup granulated sugar

¼ teaspoon salt

3 tablespoons cornstarch

2 tablespoons unsalted butter, at room temperature

½ teaspoon pure vanilla extract

• **In a large saucepan,** combine milk and vanilla bean. Over medium heat, bring mixture just to a simmer, but don't let it boil. Remove pan from heat. Pull out vanilla bean, and using the back of a small knife, scrape any remaining seeds into the milk.

• **In a large bowl,** whisk together egg, egg yolks, sugar, and salt until mixture lightens in color, about 1 minute. Whisk in cornstarch. Slowly whisk in milk until well blended. Pour mixture back into saucepan, set over low heat, and stir constantly until mixture is very thick and just beginning to boil, about 5 minutes.

• **Pour mixture into a blender.** Add butter and vanilla extract and blend on high speed for 1 minute. Use immediately, or transfer to a clean bowl, cover the surface with a sheet of plastic wrap, and refrigerate for up to 3 days.

continued

MODERN VANILLA PASTRY CREAM, CONT.

Vanilla pastry cream is perfect for layering in crusts for fruit tarts. And with a few small tweaks, you can transform it for desserts like Vanilla Cream Pie (page 71) or layer it with crisp sheets of puff pastry for an irresistible Australian Vanilla Slice (page 133).

Viva Vanilla!

Crème Anglaise: Make this classic, silky vanilla sauce with a few easy changes to the above recipe. Omit the cornstarch and butter. After whisking the hot milk into the egg mixture, return the mixture to the saucepan and cook, whisking constantly, over low heat until mixture thickens and coats the back of a spoon (do not let it bubble, or the eggs will begin to scramble). Transfer to a blender, add the vanilla extract, and blend until smooth. Crème Anglaise is perfect with fruits of all sorts and as the base of dreamy desserts like Floating Islands (page 131).

Crème Brûlée: Omit the cornstarch and the butter. After whisking the hot milk into the egg mixture, transfer mixture to the blender, add the vanilla extract, and blend for 1 minute. Place 6 1-cup ramekins on a clean dish towel laid in a roasting pan. Spoon custard into ramekins and pour enough boiling water into the pan to come halfway up the sides of the ramekins. Bake until custards are just set, 50 to 60 minutes. Let cool at room temperature for 1 hour, then cover and refrigerate overnight. When you're ready to serve, generously sprinkle each custard with about 1½ teaspoons Vanilla Sugar (page 69). Use a kitchen torch to caramelize the sugar until it is bubbling and deep amber.

SWEET VANILLA WHIPPED CREAM

There's not a whole lot on this great Earth that can't be improved with a dollop of freshly whipped cream, yes? A touch of sugar and a hit of vanilla turn this delightful creation into something extra-special. To ensure sweet, whipped success, throw your metal mixing bowl and beaters in the freezer; they should be cold before you start. Choose your bowl thoughtfully: cream typically doubles in volume when whipped.

For 1 cup heavy cream, I start with about 1 tablespoon confectioners' sugar (more or less, depending on the sweetness of the dish with which it will be served) and ½ teaspoon pure vanilla extract or, for a beautiful smattering of flecks, vanilla bean paste (this can be adjusted to taste). Whip on high speed just until soft peaks form, being careful not to overwhip—loosely whipped cream is always more luxurious than cream that's been whipped too long. *Makes 2 cups*

❋ For Boozy Vanilla Whipped Cream, add a couple teaspoons of your favorite vanilla-infused liquor (see page 151); bourbon is excellent. However you flavor it, whipped cream is always best served as soon as possible.

VANILLA BEAN BOWLS

When I throw a dinner party, I'm all about blowing minds and taking names. This little dessert presentation trick is one of my favorites. Edible dishes, people! All you need are several bars of high-quality white chocolate, whole vanilla beans, and balloons.

At least 8 ounces chopped white chocolate
(you'll need at least 2 ounces per bowl,
depending on their size)
Caviar of ½ to 1 vanilla bean

In a heatproof bowl set over a pan of simmering water, melt white chocolate gently over medium-low heat, stirring often. Stir in vanilla caviar. Let white chocolate cool until warm to the touch.

Meanwhile, blow up 4 balloons to serve as your molds. You can make them as big or small as you like; I prefer balloons with an 11-inch diameter maximum. Inflate each one about halfway to create a mold about 5 inches in diameter at the widest point (water-balloon-size balloons, although adorable, are thinner and tend to pop when they make contact with even slightly warm white chocolate).

Line 2 baking sheets with parchment paper. Lightly coat each balloon with nonstick cooking spray and lightly spray the parchment, too. Holding a balloon by its tied end, dip the bottom into the melted white chocolate and roll it from side to side to coat the surface about 3 to 4 inches up the side (irregular edges are charming!).

Alternatively, you can dip the balloon and then use a spatula to spread the white chocolate, creating attractive swirls and textures on the sides of the bowl. Set dipped balloons on prepared sheets and freeze or refrigerate until set. Pop balloons with scissors and then carefully peel them away from the bowls. Chill bowls until ready to serve; fill with whipped cream and seasonal fruits. *Makes 4 bowls*

FLOATING ISLANDS

Traditionally, this dreamboat of a dessert calls for the meringue "islands" to be either baked in a water bath or poached in milk, and the finished product is drizzled with caramel. Here, I bake the meringues, skip the caramel, and sprinkle everything with turbinado sugar for sparkle, caramelized flavor, and a bit of crunch against the creamy vanilla sauce and pillowy meringues.

4 large egg whites, at room temperature

¼ teaspoon cream of tartar

⅛ teaspoon salt

¼ cup granulated sugar

1 teaspoon pure vanilla extract

Turbinado sugar, for sprinkling

1 batch Crème Anglaise (page 126)

• **Position a rack in the center of the oven** and preheat oven to 300°F. Line a baking sheet with parchment paper.

• **In the bowl of a stand mixer** fitted with the whisk attachment, beat egg whites, cream of tartar, and salt medium-high speed until mixture holds soft peaks. Slowly add sugar and continue beating until mixture is glossy and holds stiff peaks. Beat in vanilla extract. Scoop ¼-cup mounds of meringue onto prepared baking sheet; you should have 12 total. Sprinkle each meringue with turbinado sugar. Bake until meringues are slightly puffed and just beginning to turn golden in spots, about 15 minutes. Transfer baking sheet to a wire rack and let meringues cool completely on sheet.

• **Ladle about ½ cup Crème Anglaise** into each of 6 wide, shallow bowls. Float 2 meringues on each puddle of custard and serve immediately.

Although you should assemble this delicate dessert immediately before serving, both the meringues and the custard can be prepared in advance. Make the custard up to 2 days before and store tightly covered in the refrigerator. The meringues can stand for up to 3 hours before assembling and serving the dessert.

NUTTY VANILLA SPREAD

4 ounces roasted, salted macadamia nuts

4 ounces blanched slivered almonds

2 teaspoons pure vanilla extract

⅔ cup whole milk

1 vanilla bean, split lengthwise

14 ounces white chocolate, chopped

Pinch salt (optional)

This dream concoction is essentially vanilla Nutella. Oh, yes. It's awesome on thick slices of toast, in a cookie sandwich, or straight off a spoon.

• **In the bowl of a food processor,** process nuts and vanilla extract until fine, about 2 minutes.

• **In a small saucepan over medium heat,** warm milk and vanilla bean until just about to boil. Remove vanilla bean and scrape any remaining caviar into milk. Pour milk over white chocolate and let stand for 5 minutes, then whisk until white chocolate is melted and mixture is smooth. Scrape into food processor and process with the nut mixture until it reaches the consistency you desire. Taste for salt, adding a pinch if necessary (you may not need any at all, as most packaged macadamia nuts are quite salty). Pour the spread into 4 clean half-pint jars and screw the lids on tight. Store in the refrigerator for up to 4 weeks.

This recipe makes more than the average person might consume in a month (not that I have any trouble), so package portions in pretty little jars for a unique edible gift. Spread the vanilla, spread the love, and make friends for life!

AUSTRALIAN VANILLA SLICE

Serves
9 to 12

This delicate pastry is an Australian classic that's usually made with store-bought custard powder, though here the filling is made from scratch. The marriage of flaky, buttery pastry and creamy filling is simply divine. For an extra-sweet kick, replace the confectioners' sugar with a drizzle of glaze, like the one used for Glazed Vanilla Bean Doughnuts (page 41).

2 sheets puff pastry (from 1 17.3-ounce box)

⅓ cup heavy cream, well-chilled

1 batch Modern Vanilla Pastry Cream (page 125), made with 5½ tablespoons cornstarch

Confectioners' sugar, for dusting

• **Position oven racks in the upper and lower thirds** of the oven and preheat oven to 400°F. Line a large baking sheet with parchment paper or a silicone baking mat. Line an 8- or 9-inch square baking pan with two perpendicular sheets of plastic wrap that are 5 or 6 inches longer than the pan, so that there is a bit of overhang on all sides.

• **Unfold puff pastry sheets** and place them side by side on prepared baking sheet. Prick all over with a fork, making sure to poke all the way through pastry. Place a second baking sheet on top of the pastry (this will ensure pastry won't puff too much while baking).

• **Bake until pastry is lightly golden,** about 20 minutes, rotating 180 degrees halfway through baking. Remove the top baking sheet and continue to bake until pastry is golden and crisp, about 5 minutes more. Remove the pastry sheets to a wire rack to cool completely.

• **In a small bowl,** beat cream with a hand mixer until it holds firm peaks. Gently stir half of the whipped cream into the pastry cream to lighten it, then carefully fold in the remaining whipped cream until smooth.

continued

AUSTRALIAN VANILLA SLICE, CONT.

• **To assemble,** lay 1 pastry sheet in the bottom of prepared square pan (you may need to trim the edges a bit to make it fit). Layer vanilla filling evenly over the pastry. Top with the second sheet of pastry, trimming if necessary. Fold the plastic wrap up and over the top to cover pastry. Refrigerate for at least 6 hours.

• **To serve,** use the plastic wrap to help you pull the slab out of the pan and place it on a cutting board. Dust the top generously with confectioners' sugar and slice into pieces.

FAVORITE VANILLA ICE CREAM

When it comes to desserts, what's more classic than a scoop of vanilla ice cream? The unexpected addition of sour cream makes this recipe truly crave-worthy.

2 cups whole milk

½ cup heavy cream

6 large egg yolks

1 cup granulated sugar

⅛ teaspoon salt

1 vanilla bean, split lengthwise

½ cup sour cream

2 teaspoons pure vanilla extract

• **In a blender, combine** milk, cream, egg yolks, sugar, and salt. Blend until smooth and slightly aerated, about 1 minute. Transfer to a medium saucepan over medium heat and add vanilla bean. Cook, stirring often and scraping the bottom of the pan, until mixture has thickened and coats the back of a spoon; if you run your finger through the coating on the spoon, a track should remain. Remove vanilla bean and scrape remaining caviar into pan.

• **Pour custard through a sieve** into a large bowl nested in an ice bath. Stir until custard is cool to the touch. Wash and dry the blender pitcher and pour custard into it. Add sour cream and vanilla extract and blend for 1 minute. Pour mixture back into the large bowl, cover tightly, and refrigerate for at least 6 hours or preferably overnight. Pour into an ice-cream maker and churn according to the manufacturer's instructions. Transfer to an airtight container and freeze until firm.

This is the sort of recipe that works well with vanilla of any origin. Because you're using both a whole bean and an extract, you can combine two different places of origin and make your own signature blend. I love using a Tahitian bean and Mexican extract.

Favorite Vanilla Ice Cream, page 135,
and White Hot Fudge

WHITE HOT FUDGE

This creamy, sticky, sweet sauce is the vanilla version of the classic ice-cream topping. Packed in a sweet little jar, it makes a great edible gift.

• **In a medium heatproof bowl,** combine all ingredients except vanilla bean paste. Set bowl over a saucepan of simmering water and stir mixture occasionally until it is completely smooth and the white chocolate is melted. Remove bowl from heat and stir in vanilla bean paste.

• **Let cool for 5 minutes** and then serving warm over ice cream. Store leftovers in an airtight container in the refrigerator for up to 1 week; rewarm gently before serving.

Makes
1½ cups

1 7.5-ounce jar marshmallow crème

3 ounces white chocolate, chopped

¼ cup light corn syrup

2 tablespoons heavy cream

¼ teaspoon salt

1 teaspoon vanilla bean paste

1¾ cups heavy cream, chilled

¾ cup granulated sugar, divided

2 teaspoons pure vanilla extract

2 teaspoons vanilla bean paste

3 large eggs, separated, plus 1 large egg white

¼ teaspoon salt

VANILLA BEAN SEMIFREDDO

Semifreddo **is Italian for "half cold," but what it really means is a reason to eat an entire hunk of something that resembles softened ice cream. Because it's not overwhelmingly chilled, it makes for the most wonderful vehicle for vanilla, melting quickly over your tongue as soon as you take a bite.**

• **Line a 9-by-5-by-3-inch loaf pan** with two perpendicular sheets of plastic wrap, leaving at least 3 inches of overhang on all sides.

• **Pour cream into a large bowl** with 7 tablespoons of the sugar, vanilla extract, and vanilla bean paste. With a hand mixer, whip cream until it holds firm peaks. Cover and refrigerate while you prepare the rest of the recipe. Clean beaters thoroughly.

• **Place egg whites in a medium bowl** with 3 tablespoons of the sugar and salt. Beat whites until they hold firm peaks; set aside. In another medium bowl, beat egg yolks and the remaining 2 tablespoons sugar until yolks are noticeably paler in color and thickened. Gently fold about a quarter of the whipped whites into yolks to lighten them and then carefully fold in the remaining whites.

• **Add egg mixture to the whipped cream** and fold gently to combine. Scrape into prepared pan and smooth the top with a spatula (it should come right up to the top of the pan). Fold the plastic wrap up and over the top, covering it completely. Freeze for at least 8 hours or overnight.

• **To serve,** invert the semifreddo onto a serving platter, remove plastic wrap, and slice into 1-inch-thick slices.

Viva Vanilla!

Vanilla-Caramel Semifreddo: Replacing the granulated sugar with a caramelized sugar powder punches up the flavor of this frozen dessert. Line a baking sheet with a lightly oiled piece of foil or a silicone baking mat. In a small saucepan, combine ¾ cup granulated sugar, 2 tablespoons water, and a pinch of salt. Cook over high heat, stirring gently, just until sugar begins to dissolve (from this point on, don't stir the sugar syrup). Continue cooking, gently swirling the pan occasionally, until the syrup is deep amber. Pour immediately onto prepared baking sheet and let harden. Break caramel into several pieces, place in the bowl of a food processor, and grind to a fine powder. Add to the cream before whipping and proceed with the rest of the original recipe.

COCONUT AND VANILLA BEAN ICE POPS

*Makes
about 6
3-ounce
pops*

Few things are more perfectly paired than vanilla beans and warm milk, but creamy coconut milk is a delicious companion for vanilla. This recipe is the antithesis of those freezer-burned fudge pops from the grocery store.

1 14-ounce can full-fat coconut milk

½ vanilla bean, split lengthwise and caviar scraped

3 to 4 tablespoons granulated sugar, to taste

Pinch salt

• **In a small saucepan over medium heat,** whisk together coconut milk, vanilla bean pod, vanilla caviar, sugar, and salt. Cook, stirring occasionally, until mixture just begins to bubble; remove from heat (do not boil). Cover and let steep for at least 1 hour.

• **Remove the vanilla pod** and scrape any remaining caviar into pan. Whisk mixture to blend.

• **Transfer mixture** to a large measuring cup for easy pouring and pour into ice-pop molds. Freeze until firm.

Look for a good-quality full-fat coconut milk, not one labeled "light." The best kinds are usually found in the Asian-foods aisle of the supermarket.

DRINKS

From the creamy and sweet to the floral and refreshing, vanilla adds depth and complexity to a surprising number of drinkable creations. Of all of the recipes in this book, these are the ones that let your inner culinary mad scientist come alive. So roll up your sleeves, make your own vanilla-infused syrups and liquors, and tweak these formulas to your liking. What could be more satisfying than vanilla made quaffable?

VANILLA EGG CREAM

*Makes 1
egg cream*

If you're a **New Yorker** of a certain age, the egg cream is likely an essential part of your personal fabric. If you've never had one, you might be surprised to learn that it doesn't contain any eggs. (The origins of the name are hotly debated.) Traditionally, an egg cream is made with whole milk and chocolate syrup, but since vanilla simple syrup is thinner than chocolate syrup, I re-create the creaminess of the original by using half-and-half instead of milk. I offer some general suggestions for amounts—everything can be adjusted to your tastes.

1½ to 2 ounces Vanilla Simple Syrup (page 146)

2 to 2½ ounces half-and-half

8 to 10 ounces club soda or seltzer*

> * *Freshly opened bottled soda will yield good results, but in homemade soda fountain drinks like this I like to use a soda siphon (available at beverage stores and online) to get extra fizz and a super foamy top.*

• **In a tall glass (a pint glass works well),** stir together vanilla syrup and half-and-half. Begin pouring club soda in a slow stream down the side of the glass, stirring to encourage the drink to bubble up, until the foam reaches the top of the glass. Serve immediately.

The proportion of ingredients can be adjusted to your liking. To serve a crowd, set out all the egg cream ingredients and let your party guests be the masters of their own tasty beverages.

Viva Vanilla!

Vanilla Italian Soda: Omit the half-and-half, increase the simple syrup and soda to taste, and make a refreshingly fizzy vanilla beverage. For a bit of creaminess, top with a dollop of Sweet Vanilla Whipped Cream (page 127).

HOMEMADE VANILLA
SIMPLE SYRUP

I'm a modern girl. Sure, I love making things from scratch, but I am also a fan of convenience and have no problem seeking out a store-bought item to help make life a little easier. Unless, that is, said store-bought item is exorbitantly expensive and can be made in minutes at home (and tastes better to boot). Take vanilla syrup, for example. The fancy stuff you see in coffeeshops and upscale bars? Turns out it's not so fancy after all, and it often tastes artificial. Vanilla Simple Syrup, on the other hand, is unbelievably tasty and easy to make with fresh vanilla beans. Here's the formula:

1 cup granulated sugar
1 cup water
1 vanilla bean, split lengthwise

Combine sugar and water in a small saucepan over high heat, stirring gently. Bring to a boil and boil for 1 minute, just long enough for mixture to turn clear and sugar to dissolve completely. Let syrup cool in the pan for 10 minutes. Place vanilla bean in a lidded glass jar or other heatproof container and pour syrup over the bean. Cover and let steep in the refrigerator for at least 1 day before using. *Makes 2 cups*

VANILLA MARTINI

This drink is a real chameleon. By playing with the amounts of vodka and simple syrup but keeping the amount of half-and-half the same, you can make this drink be everything from a boozy wonder to the sort of holiday dessert drink that creeps up on you and goes down way too easy.

• **Pour vanilla sugar onto a plate.** Dampen the rim of a martini glass with water. Dip rim in vanilla sugar and roll to coat.

• **Combine vanilla, vodka, half-and-half, and vanilla simple syrup** over ice in a cocktail shaker. Shake vigorously until chilled. Strain into sugar-rimmed glass and serve immediately.

Makes 1 martini

Several tablespoons Vanilla Sugar (page 69)

2 to 2½ ounces vanilla-infused vodka (page 151)

1 ounce half-and-half

1 to 1½ ounces Vanilla Simple Syrup (page 146)

VANILLA MOJITO

A standard mojito, with its blend of rum, sugar, and fresh mint leaves, is perfectly refreshing on its own. But something magical happens when you infuse it with vanilla—the mint brings out some of vanilla's more subtle, herbal qualities.

• **In a tall, narrow glass,** combine rum, vanilla simple syrup, and lime juice. Add mint leaves and use a muddler to crush leaves into the liquid. Stir in club soda, add ice, and serve immediately.

For extra sweet vanilla sparkle, rim the glass with Vanilla Sugar (page 69) before adding the ingredients.

1½ to 2 ounces vanilla-infused light rum (page 151)

1 ounce Vanilla Simple Syrup (page 146)

1 tablespoon freshly squeezed lime juice

1 big handful fresh mint leaves (about 10 to 12 large leaves)

2 ounces club soda or seltzer

HOMEMADE VANILLA-INFUSED LIQUORS

Infusing liquors with delicious flavors is a simple way to make moderately priced booze shine—and fancy up your next cocktail. And vanilla beans are one of the easiest (not to mention the most delicious) ingredients to use.

Clear, neutral-flavored liquors such as vodka and light rum are a good foundation for Madagascar vanilla; this variety's milder notes really sing in a drink like a martini or mojito (see pages 147 and 149). But you can infuse more strongly flavored liquors, too. Using the tasting notes beginning on page 19 as your guide, experiment with some exciting flavor pairings. For instance, a smoky Scotch would be a great candidate for infusing with Indian vanilla, and brandy would welcome a vanilla that has hints of fruit, such as Tahitian. If you're feeling really bold, try infusing port with vanilla from Uganda, which typically has winey, plummy notes.

All you need is a jar or bottle with a tight-fitting lid, a few vanilla beans, and your favorite booze. For every 8 ounces or so of liquor, use 1 whole bean, split lengthwise. Place the split bean in the container, add liquor, and cap it tightly. Let liquor infuse for about 3 to 5 days, depending on the flavor intensity you want. Then, remove the bean (otherwise, your booze will turn into vanilla extract!). If you want to infuse an entire bottle of liquor with vanilla flavor, simply open it, drop in the split beans, and recap it. Cheers!

2 cups raw almonds*

1 tablespoon light agave
nectar** or honey

1¼ teaspoons pure
vanilla extract

Pinch salt

*Play with the ratio of almonds
to water if you want a richer or
thinner almond milk; you can
also add more or less sweetener
to taste. Try a little cinnamon,
nutmeg, cardamom, or a
combination of all three for
extra zing.

** Like corn syrup and brown
sugar, agave nectar comes in
light and dark varieties. Light
agave is ideal for beverage
recipes like this one, because
it lets the vanilla flavor sing.

VANILLA ALMOND MILK

**Once upon a time, I completed three days of a
juice fast. For a food-obsessed person like myself,
three days of nothing but juices (no matter how
health-giving and delicious they were) was, in
short, uncomfortable. But there was a bright spot
in the whole experience: a nightly almond drink
that was so creamy, satiating, and fantastically
flavored with vanilla that it could've passed
for melted Häagen-Dazs. (Well, that may be a
starvation-induced hallucination, but it was
mighty tasty.) Soon after, I started making my
own version at home. It's delicious hot or cold.**

• **In a medium saucepan** over high heat, combine almonds
with 1½ cups water. Bring to a boil. Boil for 3 minutes. Drain
almonds and spread in an even layer on a paper-towel-lined
surface to cool. With your fingertips slip off and discard the
skins and then place almonds in the pitcher of a blender with
4 cups water, agave nectar, vanilla extract, and salt. Blend
on high power until mixture is creamy and opaque white and
almonds are pulverized.

• **Line a fine-mesh sieve** with a single layer of paper towel
or cheesecloth. Set sieve over a 1-quart lidded container. Pour
almond mixture through sieve, pressing gently on the almond
solids to extract as much milk as possible. Close container
tightly and store in the refrigerator for up to 2 weeks. Shake
well before serving.

**After you've strained the milk, don't toss those
almond solids! Once patted dry, they can be
folded into all sorts of recipes, from cookies to
quickbreads to homemade granola.**

FRUITY VANILLA ICED TEA

This ambrosial concoction is about as Lady Beverage as you can get. I love matching Tahitian vanilla with any number of fruit-flavored teas, especially ones flavored with berry, citrus, or peach.

4 unsweetened fruit-flavored tea bags*

½ vanilla bean, split lengthwise

Vanilla Simple Syrup (page 146), to taste

* *There are a myriad of unsweetened, fruit-flavored tea bags on the market, like those by Celestial Seasonings.*

• **In a medium saucepan** or teakettle over high heat, bring 4 cups water to a boil. Remove from heat, add tea bags and vanilla bean, and cover tightly. Steep for 30 minutes. Remove vanilla bean and scrape any remaining caviar into tea, discarding the pod. Strain tea into a heatproof pitcher and refrigerate until cold, about 2 hours. Serve over ice, sweetened to taste with vanilla simple syrup.

MALTED WHITE HOT CHOCOLATE

Give traditional hot chocolate a run for its money with this lush, rich vanilla version. Serve in large mugs for a drinkable dessert or pour into espresso cups or shot glasses with mini marshmallows for daintier dinner-party potables.

- 1 cup whole milk
- 1 cup half-and-half
- 3 ounces white chocolate, chopped
- ⅛ teaspoon salt
- ¼ cup malted milk powder
- 1 teaspoon pure vanilla extract or vanilla bean paste

• **Combine milk, half-and-half, white chocolate,** and salt in a medium saucepan. Stir over medium-low heat until white chocolate is melted and mixture is just becoming hot to the touch. Transfer mixture to a blender and add malted milk powder. Cover tightly and blend for 60 seconds. Pour mixture back into saucepan and reheat over low heat just until hot (don't let it boil). Stir in vanilla extract or vanilla bean paste. Serve immediately.

The Vanilla Bean Marshmallows on page 99 are a natural pairing.

RESOURCES

Even though you can buy good vanilla products in many markets and specialty stores, it's tough to find a deal when you're buying retail. I love purchasing vanilla in bulk, and often do so online for great prices and selection, not to mention better access to some of the more obscure origins.

Beanilla Trading Company

(888) 261-3384

Beanilla.com

A wonderful little company based in Michigan, these people know and love vanilla like no one else. Their wide range of whole beans, pastes, powders, and extracts kick-started my vanilla obsession. In addition to offering a slew of origins in all forms, they make their own heavenly blend of vanilla extract, all at a fair price.

Vanilla-Saffron Imports

(415) 648-8990

Saffron.com

This small but mighty company is located in the Mission district of San Francisco. These folks deal solely with the world's two most expensive spices. Their knowledge of and passion for vanilla is outstanding. The selection and prices are terrific, and the shipping is lightning fast.

Culinary District

(877) 641-2661

CulinaryDistrict.com

I frequent this website not just for top-notch vanilla products in bulk, but for all sorts of kitchen gear and high-quality baking ingredients. I order online when I'm at home in San Francisco, but when I'm visiting Los Angeles, I always hit up Surfas, the awe-inspiring brick-and-mortar location for Culinary District's goods.

The Vanilla.COMpany

(831) 476-9111

Vanilla.com

Patricia Rain is known as the "Vanilla Queen" and has dedicated years to global adventures and research in the world of vanilla. She is part owner of this wonderful site that offers a mind-boggling amount of vanilla information, as well as a carefully curated online shop.

INDEX